# Listening Inside Out

# Listening Inside Out

## Conversations with Twentysomethings About Faith, Culture, and the Church

David and Rhonda Kyncl
with Jeff Edmondson

BEACON HILL PRESS
OF KANSAS CITY

ISBN 978-0-8341-2369-4

Printed in the United States of America

Cover Design: Brandon Hill
Interior Design: Sharon Page

**Library of Congress Cataloging-in-Publication Data**

Kyncl, David, 1960-
    Listening inside out : conversations with twentysomethings about faith, culture, and the church /
David and Rhonda Kyncl with Jeff Edmondson.
        p. cm.
    Includes bibliographical references.
    ISBN 978-0-8341-2369-4 (pbk.)
    1. Church of the Nazarene. 2. Generation Y—Religious life. 3. Church work with young adults.
I. Kyncl, Rhonda, 1964- II. Edmondson, Jeff, 1966- III. Title.

    BX8699.N35K96 2008
    287.9'90842—dc22

                                                                                2008038849

10 9 8 7 6 5 4 3 2 1

# Contents

# Preface

This is a book of conversations with twentysomethings who are a part of the generation known as the Millennials, or Generation Y.[1] Like a photo album, this book is a series of conversational snapshots between young men and women, with each having his or her own unique DNA and personality. They are voices from secular and Nazarene schools, as well as some individuals who have already launched careers in the working world. Though the individuals are diverse, the purpose of this book—and the coming together in conversation—remains the same: Is there something emerging from these conversations that can help us form a more accurate view of the church? Lean in and listen: What is it that God is doing among them? How can we see the world through their eyes?

Under the leadership of Tom Nees, the vision was cast for a way to engage hundreds of ministry-minded young people in a dialogue about faith, culture, and the church. Nees wrote to the presidents of nine Nazarene colleges and universities and encouraged them to support a "once in a life-time experience for college students exploring a call to volunteer or a career in ministry and missions."[2] Presidents authorized the financial support for transportation so that students could attend the conference, and Dr. Nees's department provided complementary housing. Nees hoped, along with other denominational leaders, that the conference would be a place where individuals would experience a renewed call to ministry.

The vision for this conference included recruiting and supporting Nazarene students and graduates to cities like Montreal, Philadelphia,

Cleveland, and Chicago. Their new role in these locations would be to help establish mission projects. But, though these details seemed to work out, the question still lingered: Could an investment in youth inspire missional impact? As Tom Nees wrote in an e-mail, "What would it take from our end to design denominational strategies that would stir up the imagination and vision of students?"[3]

The leaders of the conference developed thirty questions to ask students who attended the conference. The questions were designed with a listening component, so that we, as a church, would be better equipped to crack the code of understanding the current postmodern culture. The students candidly responded to the opportunity to express their thoughts. (You may find the thirty questions in the Appendix at back of this book.)

When you read through this book, ask questions of the text. Ask the *Why?* questions, and discover the threads that link this culture with previous cultures or movements. Above all else, keep conversations going within your small group or local faith community. Turn these snapshots of conversations into an ongoing dialogue.

—Mike Stipp
Clergy Development

*Technical note:* The interviews placed at the beginning of each chapter were conducted by Jeff Edmondson. Thus, the voice of interviewer in each will always be the "voice" of Jeff.

## Introduction
# The Challenge

*Twentysomethings.* In the church, they are the ones who bring a sense of freshness to congregations. They introduce new ideas and make us feel young again. If a local church has a large number of them, we often think that church must be pretty healthy. We swell with pride as we point toward them and say, "Look at our young adult group. Aren't they great? God is really working in our church." It is as if having a strong representation of twentysomethings in a congregation means that God is pouring out His blessings. And in many ways, that may be true.

Twentysomethings challenge us with their new ideas. We love it when they ask spiritual questions, knowing they are working through their faith and that the Spirit is moving in their lives. We see their involvement in ministry opportunities as a sign that God is shaping them into the Christians He wants them to be. It's exciting. It's motivating.

Furthermore, it is in these twentysomething years that leadership begins to cultivate for the future of our congregations. While modern science continues to extend the life expectancy of the average North American, there's no pill or procedure to ensure the stability of any local church's management in the distant years. So through mentoring relationships with young adults we craft the continued hope for the future.

On the other hand, there can be downsides to having the young adult crowd our pews. For the church treasurer, the most obvious issue is that they don't always tithe—or give anything. From a strictly human and financial perspective, it doesn't make sense to invest in a group that doesn't significantly participate in the financial responsibilities of the church. Of course, that is an absurd statement to make. But it would be a lie to say that thought has never passed through the minds of those who have exposure to the church members' giving records.

Young adults and students tend to question our doctrines and our theology, often at the most inopportune moments. They think differently than the established church does. They are very postmodern thinkers, dissecting established icons of truth and maybe even forming their own truth from many different sources.

Because teenagers may easily view young adults as role models, involving them in youth ministry can be a risky business. What messages will be sent to impressionable teens if their young adult leaders question our doctrine or casually engage in activities that have traditionally been viewed as contrary to the Way? If they smoke, participate in social drinking, or espouse philosophies contrary to our traditions, what is the potential spiritual damage to our youth groups or children's ministries?

For most people, the college years were marked by some level of questioning the traditions in which they were raised. As a society, college years are simply a part of stretching one's wings and launching into adulthood. But that process is often pockmarked with poor decisions because of inexperience, immaturity, or the lack of resources. These poor decisions are life lessons, to be sure. But moving through this life-lesson process can be rocky and turbulent. Is there a ministry liability if we put college-aged individuals in places of responsibility?

Undoubtedly, those concerns would have unanimous agreement as absurd. Of course we want young adults in our churches and engaged in the life of the church. Of course there is a spiritual liability that is risked in placing them in leadership positions. But there is no more risk than that of any given person being in a leadership position in the church. Christians are human, after all, and are therefore fallible.

But even so, though the church dearly loves having students and young adults in its congregations, it does not rely heavily on this group. There is a strong desire to have them entrenched in each congregation, but their input is minimized. Instead, the church adopts a wait-and-see attitude. Possibly, this is a method of protectionism—just in case the most well-intentioned efforts don't pan out. Some leaders might go so far as to state that it is unwise to put faith in what is proven to be unstable. For those readers who are in their twenties, that last statement is likely offensive. But those readers are also likely to agree that their opinions are often written off as inexperienced ramblings of the young.

For the readers who are pastors or lay leaders of experience—the readers who aren't twentysomethings—those statements might be uncomfortable. But, upon closer examination, they would probably be agreed upon. The ultimate question in this situation is this: is it wise to discount an age-group's voice? The church might assume the advice of young adults to be unwise because of the lack of life-experience. But, in doing so, is the church then guilty of being unwise itself?

When we observe biblical history, it's interesting how often God chose the young to speak wisdom to the old:

Didn't God speak to Joseph through dreams of what was to come? In doing so, wasn't Joseph then discounted by his own family?

Wasn't Samuel merely a boy when God came to him in His Temple, whispering his name? There God spoke to Eli through Samuel, even though Eli had closed his ears to God's voice.

Wasn't David chosen in his youth to lead Israel when Saul had abandoned God's ways for his own?

As a New Testament example, didn't Paul commission young Timothy to lead the church in Ephesus?

Maybe God's choosing to speak through those of youth was due to untainted perspectives. Maybe it was because their trust in God had not been soiled by years of experience. Though we may be unable to fathom why God so often has chosen to speak through the young of His people, it is a pattern that cannot be ignored.

So if, throughout history, God has chosen to speak through young followers, why is it that the modern church has such difficulty listening to its young adults? Or rather, has the leadership of the church become so confident in its years of experience that it does not actually *hear* when God speaks through His modern young believers?

## The Flip Side

There is a growing body of evidence that postmoderns in their twenties are dissatisfied with the church. The nation is hearing this by way of statistical studies and surveys. Research groups such as the Barna Group, The Center for Parent and Youth Understanding, Focus on the Family, and many others have spent years looking at polls, cultural changes, and many other factors that indicate this fact. According to some research, postmodern believers see the church as almost irrelevant.[4] The frustration the church faces is that it seems as though we are blind to the reasons why this generation is so dissatisfied with the church. And if we are blind to it, how can the church even know how to address their dissatisfaction?

But there is another, deeper issue that is even more troubling. It is an issue which may be the source for the dissatisfaction felt by many in their twenties. Evidence points to the complete inadequacy of the church's ministry to young adults between graduation from youth group—a time when most young Christians are still involved in church—and graduation from college—when, according to a Barna research poll, 61 percent of young adults give up on the church all together.[4] Clearly, the church is not engaging the young adult generation in a way that seems significant. And if not in a significant manner, how much less is the church engaging them using a relevant methodology?

Possibly, the answer is pretty simple. Maybe the reason behind their lack of satisfaction is that they've been expressing *why* all along, but the church just hasn't been listening. Maybe God has been speaking through them all along—as He has throughout history. How much more frustrating can it be to have something important to say, only to continually be faced with people who are closed off to what needs to be said?

## How It All Started

Haunted by this reality, leaders of the Church of the Nazarene decided to purposefully begin listening to what this younger generation had to say. The challenge was to engage the postmodern generations in a church that has become increasingly irrelevant in the eyes of its postmodern twentysomethings.

As part of the effort to meet this challenge, representatives of the Church of the Nazarene began a conversation with twentysomethings. These church representatives were comprised of men and women who deeply care about the postmodern generations, and who work with them in various capacities—Christian higher education, secular higher education, singles ministries, young adult ministries, etc. To further the conversation, students from various private and public colleges and universities from across the U.S. and Canada were invited to participate in a dialogue that would be held at the International M7 Conference in Kansas City in February of 2007. The goal was to have at least four hundred students in attendance, those four hundred being representatives of the millennial generation. They identified six themes (or topics) for this conversation and asked leaders in the Church of the Nazarene who worked with the young adult population to facilitate roundtable discussions that would occur on the last two days of the conference. The point was to have face-to-face discussions about the issues confronting this generation and the church. Specifically, the hope was to hear what twentysomethings have to say about the church and its ministry to postmoderns and millenials.

The students came.

The moderators were given the list of discussion topics.[5]

And the conversations began.

## Why This Book Is Needed

Research into the millennial generation seems to suggest that engagement and interest in spirituality is at an all-time high. The Higher Education Research Institute at UCLA took a survey in 2003 of over 112,000 first-year students entering over 230 colleges and universities across the nation. The study found that 83 percent of the participants believe in the sacredness of life, and 80 percent have an interest in spirituality. In addition, 76 percent said they "search for meaning/purpose in life," while 74 percent discuss the meaning of life with their friends; 64 percent said their spirituality was a source of joy, and finally, 47 percent noted that they "seek out opportunities to help me grow spiritually."[6]

Given these numbers how does leadership juxtapose these indicators of a spiritual hunger among the majority of college students with the belief that, according to George Barna, they are leaving the church in larger numbers than ever?[7] Clearly, today's twentysomethings have a deep interest in spirituality, yet they are not finding the connection between that interest and what they see in church.

This book is an attempt to broadcast the voices of twentysomethings. What's the point of listening if what is heard is not addressed? How can the church change its methods, in light of postmodern insight, if those voices are never broadcast? The church needs to honor and respect the testimony and witness that young adults hold and, together, move forward hand-in-hand.

This idea of testimony and witness is a profound one. Those who read this book should realize the importance of the twentysomething voice as foundational to the twenty-first-century church. Perhaps the significance of testimonial voices can best be explained through biblical scholar Walter Brueggemann, an Old Testament professor at Columbia Theological Seminary. Brueggemann speaks of the implications of testimony and witness in his book *The Cadences of Home: Preaching to Exiles*. He describes testimony as first person accounts—"that is, utterance by alleged first-person witnesses who offer an account of experience that depends solely upon the trustworthiness of the witnesses, but that cannot appeal for verification either to agreed-upon *metaphysics* or to external *historical data*." The importance of this kind of utterance is immeasurable, because it actually serves a prophetic purpose. "It is, rather, originary of new reality that was not available until uttered. The testimony uttered among exiles can appeal to no answer in the back of the book, but must make its own case as best it can."[8] The goal is to allow the testimonies of this group to speak for themselves as they conjure up a new reality for the twenty-first-century church. The desire is that through listening, the church would emerge in the twenty-first century as a place of acceptance, unconditional love, and unabashed hope. With your patient and continued commitment, the leadership of the Church of the Nazarene promises to walk alongside its twentysomethings to see changes begin, and to strive toward the creation of an alternative where no young person feels abandoned by the church. This is, in the end, the only option.

It's important to note that this book is meant to incite conversations. The reader will not receive a plan of action at the conclusion of this book; to attempt to do so would be far beyond the scope of listening. And it would be pointless. Each congregation in the church faces different ministry challenges and opportunities. Each is unique. To prescribe a plan of action that would fit for all would simply not work. Rather, this book is meant to present at least some of the voices of twentysomethings, and then to challenge the readers to digest, contemplate, discuss, and formulate what needs to happen in their own ministry situations.

## How the Book Works

The chapters are organized around the issues raised during those two days of discussion at the M7 conference in February 2007. Each chapter focuses on one particular issue and begins with an interview held with a young believer in the Church of the Nazarene. Because the conversations of each roundtable discussion were too broad and fast-paced to catch and explore every opinion, it makes sense to listen to at least one voice in the conversation. Therefore, specific interviews were conducted to accomplish this purpose. Bear in mind that though the opinions of these interviewees do not necessarily reflect the opinions of all, their responses are certainly thought provoking, and are reflective—to a large extent—of this generation's opinions.

Following each interview, there is a summary of the responses from the roundtable discussions. The summary includes salient quotes that best exemplify the discussions as they occurred during the conference. These quotes are not comprehensive and do not include the names of those who voiced them. (Because of the nature of the conversations, it was impossible to record every name with every quote.) Even so, these quotes are witnesses, testimonies—though they do not represent every young adult voice in the church, they do have merit.

Following the summary of the discussion responses, each chapter contains a section dedicated to contextualizing these discussions in the twenty-first-century milieu. Each testimonial is written by an individual experiencing these issues in his or her daily life, and it offers a spiritual approach to these issues in a way that is engaging and worthy of emulation.

Finallly, there is a short "Food for Thought" paragraph which serves as a proposition of sorts, hoping to spark the reader to consider the chapter within the context of his or her own ministry.

The epilogue of the book summarizes the entire work and gives some tools for continued dialogue and thought. Again, the goal of this book is to serve as a catalyst, so that long overdue conversations will finally occur. The church cannot ignore these issues and challenges any longer. This book should become a departure point for the leaders of the churches.

May the Holy Spirit revive the church through this dialogue and its after effects. Only through the Holy Spirit can this be accomplished, and only as churches are eager to obey as He leads.

And so, "My dear brothers, take note of this: Everyone should be quick to listen, slow to speak and slow to become angry" (James 1:19).

Let the listening, and the conversations, begin.

Chapter 1
# Personal Growth

## Insights on Personal Growth

From Luke Cole & Jeff Anglin

*The casual atmosphere of a coffee shop is the perfect setting for any conversation. And so to a local coffee shop I go for a discussion on the issues of personal spiritual growth and the church's role in that growth. I am joined by two Nazarene Theological Seminary (NTS) students. Both had attended the M7 conference and had participated in the roundtable discussions, and both were eager for their voices to be heard on these issues.*

*Jeff Anglin arrives first and sits across from me, stirring a steaming cup of cappuccino and nibbling on a muffin. Out on the patio, his wavy, light brown hair flutters in the breeze. His squinting eyes size me up through metal framed glasses as the sun's glare strikes his face. As we chitchat I discover that this Midwesterner feels a call to full-time pastoral ministry with an eventual desire to become a missionary.*

*Luke Cole, another NTS student, joins us after a while. Luke, a quick-witted former probation officer hailing from Ohio, also feels called into full-time pastoral ministry. It was at the M7 conference, ironically, that he felt a call to full-time pastoral ministry.*

Not wanting to waste any time, I toss out the first thought. "What should the church be doing in the area of discipleship? How should the church be helping people with their spiritual growth?"

They look at each other momentarily, wondering which one should answer first. Then Luke dives in.

"I've always been a Nazarene. Though I've attended other denominational churches, I really like the Nazarene church. There is an established form of personal discipleship in a Nazarene church.

"I go to Central Church of the Nazarene here in Kansas City. They have a lot of programs and resources created by the Church of the Nazarene that really promote personal growth. For example, Sunday School is a huge program at our church. But really, it's sort of a hallmark for our denomination."

"Should Sunday School be changed in any way?" I ask, wanting more. "Is it effective?"

Luke thinks about this for a moment. "Well, I didn't go to school for sociology or anything like that," he replies. "But here's my personal soapbox: With today's ever-increasing advances in technology, there are a lot of factors that have torn apart a sense of community. Because of this, Sunday School and small groups and home churches become important as they bring back that sense of community and cohesion. Just a once-a-week Sunday visit to church became a little hollow for a lot of people; it wasn't enough. Not because the construct of Sunday School was bad, but because people just wanted more of a connection. They have moved to small groups because traditional Sunday School can be a little too structured." He shrugs, raises his eyebrows, and fiddles with the straps of his backpack as he looks to me for a reply of some sort.

"So you say that discipleship is more of a lifestyle, rather than sitting together going through a book? Is that what I'm hearing you say?"

"Absolutely," he responds. "I think one reason why the small group approach—which is the only alternative option to Sunday School—hasn't really worked in the past is because it's still meeting only once a week over a book, trying to learn more about the Bible instead of actively engaging in this walk of faith. We need to begin adapting discipleship into our lifestyles in very real and tangible ways. I'm all for organized Sunday School, but there definitely needs to be more of a balance.

"Education is very important. One thing that even Willow Creek admits to is that they don't teach people to read and study the Bible. Unfortunately, a lot of Sunday School is taught by an 'I think this, I think that' mind-set. I just don't really care to spend my time like that. It's good to get opinions, but let's see what the Bible really says. We need to learn how to exegete the Word into modern day application."

I roll this over in my mind. "You guys are NTS students, so you have a desire, or at least a requirement, to exegete the Word." They both laugh and mutter something about the requirement typically having more pull than the desire.

I press on. "But how does the church take an issue like theological depth and help the standard layperson, who just wants to get by on a week-to-week basis, and incite a desire in him to dig into theology?"

"I think that's the problem—we have the idea that it's OK for there to be a theological separation between clergy and laity," Luke says. "In this book called Pastor, the author very clearly lays out the functions of the pastor which are to preach, teach, pray, offer spiritual guidance—everything that we would usually attribute to the functions of a pastor. Those things are good for them to do, but they're also good for the laity to do as well. I mean, we're all the Body of Christ, right? So some pastors might read thicker books than others, but our doctrines of holiness, sanctification, the trinity—these things that we go to school to study—should not be dumbed down for laity's sake. While we might have to lend understanding to those who have not spent four years in an academic institution studying this stuff, it's not like we can—or should—dumb it down for them."

I'm intrigued now by where Luke is going with this. "So, how have the Nazarenes succeeded in teaching our doctrines?"

Setting down his coffee cup, Jeff jumps in on this one, eager to join the conversation. "Well, I think it's pretty difficult in this time period. Even the general church, the church outside of our denomination, is trying to figure out the doctrine of sanctification." He pauses and pushes a hand through his mop of hair. "I don't mean that as a slight; I mean that because it's such a respectable thing. A friend of mine said that he really respects the Nazarenes because we are willing to look at our doctrines and say 'Is this really biblical? Is this really what is true?' He said we're not trying to shove it underneath anything.

"And I think that's true, in part, because the average churchgoer doesn't know Greek or Hebrew—nor do many pastors, for that matter. So it's hard to dig down deep when trying to figure everything out. And though people might not want to go along with you on that journey, we still do our best to teach it."

Luke cuts in. "When we talk about the church adequately conveying our fundamental doctrines, there are a lot of problems in our society to consider, like pluralism and postmodernism, the emergent church—is it good, is it bad—our doctrines, what does a healthy family look like, etc," he says, leaning back in his chair. "For me it's not whether or not we've adequately addressed our doctrines. It's that there are a lot of things we just haven't adequately addressed."

"How do we change that?" I ask. "What do we need to do?"

Luke smiles at me. "Dude, I'm only twenty-four and in my first year of seminary. You want me to answer that?"

Jeff laughs also and then says, "Yeah, it's really a bigger issue than we or any one single person can answer. But there are some simple things that can be done to pass on our doctrine, like keeping ministers accountable to their study. Once you're out of seminary or school, you aren't suddenly free from ever studying again. I find that a lot of ministers end up doing nothing when it comes to studying about their faith. But the thing is, they are responsible to prepare for their role because of their congregation. A couple of district superintendents I know say that our generation will get their sermons from somewhere like Sermons.com. To me, that's just disrespectful to the call that God has placed on their lives."

"I think accountability is a good word," Luke states, nodding his agreement. "Evolutionary doctrines are rampant in our Nazarene schools right now. There are professors who don't believe in sanctification. There are Sunday School teachers in my church saying that hell isn't real. We have people in positions of authority and leadership that, to me, espouse some downright crazy, heretical types of beliefs. I can understand where a lot of that comes from. They're exploring; they're developing ideas. That's a very healthy thing to do. But when Jeff says accountability is the key, he's right—we've got a lot of people in the church holding onto some pretty nutty ideas that need to be kept in check."

I find it interesting that these two young students, whom I would have thought to be more liberal in their theology, are coming down on a more conservative side. I press on, wanting to know their thoughts on the iconic doctrines of the Church of the Nazarene. "So, regarding the ideas of holiness and sanctification, is it healthy for the church to explore what those mean and bring them into question? Or, have we settled them and don't need to question them anymore?"

"Well, I think it's healthy to explore those ideas. If we look at the Catholic church, for example, Vatican II caused the church to become so much more relevant, and not in a bad way," Jeff answers. "We began questioning the doctrines, saying, 'Seriously, what is this about?' Suddenly, nineteen hundred years after the Early Church, we decided that this is such an important issue to address. We found the need to form together a coalition of churches who saw that the Holy Spirit's movement in a person's life can be so dynamic it completely changes them beyond salvation. We found this to be so important it became the hallmark of who we are. But the key is that it's more so the question of why, rather than the question of not just believing it."

"Then the issue of holiness is still relevant?"

They look at each other for a moment, as if sharing a telepathic thought. Then Jeff shrugs and says, "Yes, it's relevant. Frankly, people in my generation find holiness to be almost like a fairy tale. They see the people in their lives who have various addictions and then combine that with what is taught at revivals or in the most rural churches (the small churches, which are the most common churches in the Church of the Nazarene) where holiness is defined as 'Come down to the altar and the Holy Spirit will, in a single moment, give this second act of grace. Just come down and it will change your parameters.' But the problem with this view of holiness is that it became so simplistic; we didn't think about real life when we considered it. And so a lot of people in my generation are thinking, This just doesn't match up with real life."

I notice that Luke wrinkles his brow in thought. "Do you agree with that, Luke?" I ask.

"No, I don't. Here's what I would say about holiness and the ability for there to be such a transformational work—beyond salvation—of the grace of God that forever changes us: We're not able to live a Christian, holy life; only Christ was able to do that. But, Christ living in us—the imminence of God living in our lives—is what makes us holy. And it's only because of that that we have holiness. That's one of the very few things that gives us relevance today."

I'm not sure he's answered the question I thought he would answer, so I make it more specific. "But do you think the church has done a good job of explaining that? Because I think that's what Jeff was saying."

"Well, yes and no . . ." Luke says, rolling the thought around in his brain.

Jeff dives in before Luke can finish. "What I mean is that there's a different understanding of the doctrine of holiness today. There was an understanding in the 1920s of what holiness meant that was different than the understanding of holiness held in the 1950s—which is even different than what we understand of it today. We have individuals like Tom Oord who are putting forth this idea of holiness as only a relationship. It's become so entrenched in a lot of conversations. But in all of my readings about the doctrine of holiness, I didn't notice that idea at all from the 1920s to the 1950s."

"What do you think, Luke?"

"A lot of that is semantics. When we read about the doctrine of holiness in the 1950s versus that of today, a lot of that is an attempt to interpret it in a language that is understandable. You read some stuff that's just fruit loops. And then you read other stuff that wows you and helps you really understand it. So I agree with Jeff, but only to a certain extent.

"When you asked the question of is it OK to question why, my answer is yes, but only to a certain degree. I think it's OK to question the doctrine of holiness and to make changes where necessary. The only point where I'm hesitant is when you hear people who are being dogmatic about a belief. But if we remove dogma from religion whatsoever, then what's there to die for? So I'm OK to call it into question, but unless there's some glaring error, then I'm OK not calling it into question."

"Do you think that's one of the issues for your generation?" I ask.

*"That we've taken away the dogma and now your generation feels like the church doesn't even know what it stands for, so why even bother?*

*"Oh yeah, that's huge,"* Luke declares. *"My wife and I recently helped start an Arabic church. The cultural differences are much more pronounced when you live within two different cultures. In the rest of the world, if they fight about religion, they are fighting about whose god is right or which book has the most authority. In America, we just explain God away. He just doesn't exist for us anymore. So yes, I do think that our lack of dogma is a major concern."*

## Roundtable Discussion Overview

As C. S. Lewis so simply wrote in *Mere Christianity*, "The Church exists for nothing else but to draw men into Christ, to make them little Christs. If they are not doing that, all the cathedrals, clergy, missions, sermons, even the Bible itself, are simply a waste of time. God became man for no other purpose."[9] Consequently, the three recurring themes that emerged from the discussion about personal growth are at first encouraging, but then critically challenging for the body of Christ. In fact, these three themes were more clearly articulated, and conversations around them exemplified more unity, than in any other topic discussed during the conference.

The first theme that rose during the discussion was that students desperately desire relationships within a faith community that are deep and lasting. This idea was also reflected in the other topics discussed during these sessions. Second, students see the value of scriptural authority and are actively pursuing lives that incorporate Scripture on a daily basis. And finally, students do not clearly understand the particular doctrinal theologies that church hierarchy has claimed as distinctive within their respective denominations.

The discussion on personal growth began with moderators posing these four questions to the roundtable participants:

- **How does the church stay connected to your generation?**

- **Is the holiness message still relevant? What is the message in your eyes?**

- **How does a Christian mature spiritually?**

- **What is the "role of authority" of Scripture?**

During this discussion, roundtable participants visited the idea of the importance of faith within a community. They particularly focused on these key relationships when discussing how the church can remain connected to their generation. Their answers predominantly reflected the desire for life mentors:

"We need somebody to invest in our lives, not just give us water on move-in day."

"I go to Sunday School now, but I want something deeper—a deeper relationship, a home fellowship, something where someone asks me, 'Hey, how are you doing?'"

"We are searching for authenticity."

"Church drops the youth after high school. Instead, they need to connect to college-age students."

"We need more invested mentors."

"There's really no college-age program, they just shuffle us into adult programs."

"Build a community where college students are valued. We need mentors to help us navigate growing up."

"We have never experienced what a true Christian community looks like."

"We need to focus on the kids as well as the youth. We need mentorship—we don't want to leave the church when relationships are formed."

"This age is drawn to non-institution. We're not interested in the big deal. It's an attitude of 'you are either in or out'—there is only one chance. First impressions are important."

It's clear from many of the comments made that the sentiments of those in the roundtable discussions are echoed in the comments by our interviewees, Luke Cole and Jeff Anglin. These students desire a community, a relationship with their local body of believers that is more of a lifestyle than just a weekly class.

As the conversations progressed during the conference, students continually returned to the notion of accountability relationships that are not forced but that occur naturally within the faith community. They voiced the desire for relationships that demand something of them and that invest in the younger children of the Body of Christ. As one student said, "I'd like more interaction with accountability from young to old—the young giving passion to the old, and the old giving wisdom to the young. This way, everyone feels needed and it becomes an accountable community and doesn't leave anyone out."

Clearly, students are seeing the importance of intergenerational communities. They are resistant to the compartmentalization of the past, where the senior adults go to their own corner, the children to theirs, and the youth to theirs. The model the students desire is the same as that described by Kenda Creasy Dean and Ron Foster in their book *The Godbearing Life.* This model, called "The One-Eared Mickey Mouse Model of Youth Ministry," shows how young people have only "marginal contact" with the entirety of the congregation. Their services, their activities, their space—everything—is completely separated from the whole life of the community.[10]

Students noted that in these generalized and compartmentalized communities, inevitably someone is left out, as has often happened with college-aged singles who no longer belong in the youth group but aren't quite ready to be members of the young married group either. "We need more merging of generations. We need to get away from the idea that you have to be 'specialized' to work with certain age-groups." Intergenerational communities would allow them to be served and to serve as well.

Perhaps the students' desire for strong mentor relationships and other mentor opportunities comes from the time and energy they spend in the Word of God. Their comments regarding the Bible show a clear grasp of the Word as authoritative and life-changing:

"Scripture has absolute authority."

"A good Christian daily submits to the Word of God. We will only grow if we do this on a daily basis."

"We should use the Bible to look at the entire nature of God, not just at what we want to see."

"I'm discovering Scripture as a story."

"Scripture speaks to us everyday; it is communication with God."

"It is the Rock of Truth, especially in such a chaotic world."

While students overwhelmingly saw the importance of having a scriptural foundation and of following the Bible for daily direction, many had critiques of how the church reflects the Word. Some students pointed out the church hasn't done a good job of contextualizing Scripture: "Has the church clarified the context of Scripture? The context is vague or greatly unknown to the general reader." Others don't see Scripture lived out in their faith communities: "Scripture would hold more authority if Christians lived it out." Finally, one student summed up the authority of Scripture in this way: "You can't understand the power of Scripture until you experience the application of it in your life."

While the discussions made it clear that students value the Word of God and are looking to it regularly for direction and guidance, their responses were not nearly as positive when discussing church doctrine. The remarks about two specific doctrinal ideas—holiness and sanctification—introduced during the roundtable discussions showed disparate opinions about the two concepts and their irrelevance and misappropriation in the lives of twentysomethings:

"We're taught definitions of holiness without learning what it really is."

"Holiness equals a byword in a sermon, but it is never explained. Pastors just don't preach it."

"We don't see role models. The character of holiness shown in others is in short supply."

"Holiness is still very relevant and important, because the Bible calls us to Christlikeness, to being different and set apart so we can reach others."

"Holiness is an appealing call toward righteousness and away from the enticements of 'self' and the world."

"We're too concerned about holiness and are therefore not connecting with people in life. For holiness to be relevant, it needs to be put into action, not just in word."

"No one understands the concept of entire sanctification."

"Is it sin management?"

"Sanctification is not used enough in this generation; it's so much more than a list of do's and don'ts."

The students represented in these pages are discernibly concerned about their individual spiritual growth. Their desire for this is confirmed by their dedication to the reading and application of Scripture to their daily lives, and by their desire for discipling relationships that encourage their spiritual development.

The diverse remarks about religious doctrine presented above could be interpreted in a number of ways. One interpretation is that they simply have not been educated on the importance of these doctrinal issues within the faith to the point of an accurate understanding. On the other hand, their disdain for such doctrinal issues may affirm their spiritual ardor. Or perhaps they see a disconnect between spirituality and organized religion—a common conception among millenials and students surveyed in some research projects.[11] It is not outside the realm of possibility that students see doctrines such as sanctification and holiness as subordinate issues where the work of personal growth is concerned.

Either way, we must again conclude that strong, intergenerational relationships within the Body of Christ would alleviate the confusion that college-aged students feel about these doctrinal issues. Through mentoring and discipling relationships, students would see the purpose of these doctrinal concepts authentically demonstrated in the lives of their mentors—if in fact such issues are critical to the daily living out of our faith. If our doctrines have become distractions to the true work of the church, then we must critically reevaluate our focus as a faith community.

## Personal Growth

By Dave Curtiss

Imagine approaching a river. You look to your left and see the river curving toward you. It is impossible to see where it has come from. Yet you see the current and know that it has changed, almost right in front of you. As your eyes move from left to right you see the change. The calm water to the left is now rocking and rolling downstream. The water has broken into turbulent white water. It is beautiful, full of energy, more broken up, and frothy.

You might think that the river had never experienced this kind of change before, that it had always run quiet and calm from its source.

But it has gone through many changes before. And it will go through many more changes before it empties into the larger tributaries downriver. It cannot go backward. No way. You couldn't move the water back upstream even if you tried with every part of your being. It continues to flow forward.

In some ways, this is the picture of change in the world and in the church in which we find ourselves. It is the picture of change that our students have articulated to us in this book. It can be unsettling, even a bit frightening, as we see change happen. Very few of us like change, but we all must deal with change throughout our entire lives. In fact, the only thing we really know about change is that everything changes.

How has the Church stayed relevant to each generation? It hasn't. It never will. The kingdom of God is not about relevancy; rather, it's about an alternate viewpoint to a temporarily established world. It is a different way of seeing and living life together, a kingdom not of this world that is both now and not yet. It is the story of God and His imprint on our life together.

These students seriously want more of God. They seek a deeper community and passion for life and others. But they simply are not interested in sustaining institutions or building monuments. They aren't interested in a life that appears holy on the outside but on the inside is betrayed by a judgmental spirit, shallow thinking, and self-centered living separate from the world God has created and is in love with. They aren't interested in separateness if it means a lack of engagement. They are not inspired by talk of devotion. Instead, they are inspired by a true devotion to what matters to God.

This generation is seeking a relevancy of the Kingdom to the world they live in. They care that the church cares about the things that are important to them—environment, slavery, brokenness, war, family, compassion, AIDS—and they care that the church either closes its eyes or opens its heart to what is really going on in the world.

The students' words in this project reflect their desire for God to be part of all of life, not just a portion. They desire a holistic approach that isn't segregated from the world but is invested, involved, and partnered with all of God's creation in bringing about the kingdom of God. A remarkably Wesleyan approach, to summarize. If there is ever a time for the Church of the Nazarene to be who we say we are, it is for such a time as this.

Is the holiness message relevant? Of course. But not if it is parsed in pietistic statements of what we don't do, as well as of the people and places we refuse to engage. We are not saved so much from something, as to something.

Students are yearning for our discussion of holiness to move from a moment in time to a life full of grace, compassion, and generative in nature. Far too often, students observe individuals in churches who give testimony to being sanctified, but yet they live a shallow, hypercritical, and hypocritical life. Our students are rejecting, and will continue to reject, any expression of holiness that is not backed up by a life filled with the love of Jesus Christ.

Christian holiness is Christlikeness and godliness. At its heart, entire sanctification is a work of grace where God restores us to His image and where His heart is found in our life and love of the Lord Jesus Christ. It is revealed in our love for Him and others, rather than in how well we can keep the rules of Christian behavior. It is revealed by how we love, and especially by how we love those whom others reject in the places where most refuse to go.

There has never been a more critical moment for the church and its people to truly live holiness in a passionate way. This is the holiness of heart and life that students yearn for. It is loving God with all of our heart, mind, and strength, and actively loving and engaging *all* of our world. It is holiness lived daily with passion and compassion.

## Food for Thought

In light of all this, how is the church to respond to the insight offered in this chapter? Has the church become stagnant in its efforts to bring people into deep relationships with a holy God? Has the church innovated its teaching methods to help believers truly understand the doctrines it is formed upon? Has it articulated those doctrines in clear, simple language so that all of its members can understand? Or has the church skirted the issue for so long that the doctrines it holds to be sacred have been lost in obscurity? How is the church to move its congregations into deeper, intergenerational relationships with each other?

All are difficult questions to answer, but all are important to grapple with.

# Chapter 2
# Lifestyle

## Insights on Lifestyles and the Church
From Matt Frye

*The phone rings on the other end, two times, then three. I'm worried I might have missed Matt as we had only a small window of opportunity to meet.*

*He answers his phone just before the fourth ring and I am greeted by his warm, cheerful voice. Matt is a young, single youth pastor in a church that reaches out to lower-income families in Medina, Ohio, a rural city situated thirty minutes south of Cleveland and twenty minutes northwest of Akron. Matt's ministry responsibilities not only include the teen department, but he also oversees the children's ministry and the growing young adult ministry in his church. Because our time is limited, and given that I've briefed him already via e-mail, I move right into our questions.*

*"So, Matt, tell me how you think the church is doing in ministering to those who have 'alternative' lifestyles."*

*"You know, that's a good topic. I think certain churches and communities do well at that, and others just don't. It's kind of a hit or miss, wherever you're at kind of thing. But I would say that most churches probably miss out on great opportunities to minister to those people."*

There is a pause on the line and I start to jump in with a new question, but Matt continues his thought before I can ask. "I think that because of the way many Christians were brought up, we have a mentality that we need to be the 'moral police' in the world. We feel the need to tell people they are wrong just because we're right rather than just loving people. But the thing is, we're all made in the image of God. None of us are better than the other. We will all come before His light one way or another, so it becomes an issue of loving people into Christianity, regardless of the lifestyle they choose, and being able to love people simply because they're made in the image of God."

"So why do you think the church has such a difficult time ministering to alternative lifestyles?" I ask. "You said most churches have a hard time doing this. Why do you think that is?"

"I think its just human nature to surround yourself with people who think like you and who agree with you. It's a lot easier. And it's common sense. Like if you were running a business—it's a lot easier to run that business when everyone's on the same page and everyone agrees with what the business stands for. You're able to push that business forward.

"I think that we've adopted that model into the church. It's kind of become our mind-set to the point that if we surround ourselves with people who agree with us and think like us, then that's what the church should look like."

"Alright, then let's say someone who is living in a lifestyle we don't condone—be it gay, heterosexual living outside of wedlock, whatever—how do we deal with that in the church?"

Matt chuckles before answering. "Well, I don't think you deal with it. I think that is something to be dealt with, in that, in the book of James, it says we all stumble in our own ways, we all have our issues, our things that keep us from being perfect. So in that regard, I don't *think it's a 'let's point our fingers and tell them to be like us' action. Instead, it's an action of us loving them and allowing God's love to challenge them and to reconcile them.*

*"Let's say a homosexual man walks into your church. The most responsible thing a church can do is love him, regardless of what lifestyle he chooses. You just love him into the Kingdom. It doesn't always mean that man is not going to be gay anymore, but that's not up to you. All we can do is love people regardless of what lifestyle they choose. Obviously, questions will arise. That gay man might ask, 'What is your stance on homosexuality?' It's OK to have a stance, but it's not OK to tell him that he is not welcome at your church, or that he can't be a part of this or that. It's about loving him and telling him that you're dealing with it too. You're loving people regardless of background, race, or orientation."*

*I want to press him further on this perspective. "Matt, what if that homosexual person wants to join the church? If he's in a lifestyle we don't condone, do we let him join anyway?"*

*"Well, yeah. I mean, I don't think it's a deal breaker. This is a really tricky question because if I say yes, then I'm saying that now we allow openly gay people to be in the community. And if I say no, then it leads to a question of what we will allow them to do.*

*I know that raises all kinds of questions either way you go. But ultimately, I say yes. What you're saying to that person is 'We love you.' His thing may be homosexuality, but someone else's thing is pornography, and someone else's is that he lies. You just have to be realistic about the fact that we all have something, and his being gay doesn't exclude him from being in the community. There is no sin greater than the other."*

*"OK, so how do we change that attitude in the church? How do we encourage the church to come at it from the perspective of open-ended love?"*

*There is static on the line, some bumping. I assume Matt is mov-ing something on his end of the connection. "Well I don't think we can do anything. That's something God has to do."*

*"But don't you think we have some sort of responsibility to help people see that?" I interrupt.*

*"Oh, sure, sure! I see what you're saying. I think the best thing we can do is to show it in our own lives, especially by belonging to a de-nomination that believes in sanctification and being dressed in the love of God. If that's true of our lives then the fruits of our love should be grace and understanding and mercy. As we claim to be Christians, as we claim to be on this journey together, then we show this change through ourselves. St. Francis of Assisi said that we are to 'Preach the gospel at all times, and if necessary, use words.' That's a power-ful thing. Why aren't we able to just embrace the love that was given to us and share that with the world—a world that needs that great love because of its alternative lifestyle? Instead, we stand on a soap-box and preach about how people really need to live. The reality is, love changes more than words will be able to."*

## Roundtable Discussion Overview

Mention the word *lifestyle* to a typical churchgoer and undoubted-ly, the issue of sexual orientation is raised. Lifestyle, as it pertains to sexuality, has become a hot topic both politically and theologically. It is bantered about by groups on the right and the left.

The questions posed during the M7 conference centered on more than this issue, however. And the answers given showed the corre-sponding desire of the students to engage the topic of lifestyle in a manner that went beyond merely sexuality.

The questions asked of the four hundred students at the round-table discussions were:

- **What is Christian purity when it comes to lifestyle and sexuality?**

- **How is a Christian lifestyle distinct from a non-Christian lifestyle?**

- **Are there behaviors that Christians need to avoid? Why?**

- **Are there behaviors that Christians need to authenticate within their lifestyle? Why?**

The first noticeable theme that arose from this discussion was that purity is an issue that reaches far beyond the challenge of abstaining from pre-marital sex. In fact, several students expressed a need for the concept of purity to be better defined and better explained to their generation and to younger generations as well. Many noted that while sexuality is not the definitive issue within purity, it is a part of the larger concept.

"Purity involves not only actions but thoughts as well."

"Sexuality is only one aspect of purity; it's dangerous to separate it out of the whole of life."

"Purity should deal with putting God first and yielding everything to Him. It is a purity of heart, not just actions."

"Purity is more than just modesty and sexuality; it's having a pure heart, mind, etc."

These ideas of purity and the desires to place emphasis on more than sexual concerns are not only refreshing, but they exist in the spirit of the ancient church. St. John of the Cross, in his now famous work *The Dark Night of the Soul,* discussed the importance of purity as a process of spiritual growth that arises after a soul has experienced spiritual gratification. It is a purity that moves beyond superficiality. "[Some] begin to do these spiritual exercises to be esteemed by others. They want others to realize how spiritual they are . . . They will beg God to take away their imperfections, but they do this only because they want to find inner peace and not for God's sake. They do not realize that if God were to take away their imperfections from them, they would probably become prouder and more presumptuous still."[12] Purity must be explained and lived in our faith communities as something that goes beyond the initial consolation offered to us early in our spiritual journeys. It must go into a deeper and deeper relationship with God Almighty.

While purity as a concept is a much more complex subject and is described by these students as more than sexual abstinence before marriage, many did affirm that sex is something that plays a role in our ideas of purity and in our efforts as believers to live lives distinct from non-Christians. Another issue that arose in the discussion about sexuality was the onslaught of media images that make sex a commodity in our culture and that assault our minds daily. Students expressed a savvy understanding of how we are all being mentally attacked by this warfare.

**"There's this idea that sex is something that can be sold, a commodity that doesn't have any meaning. It's not seen as a spiritual act."**

"In our hyper-sexualized culture, all it takes is a little hook or an Internet ad to get you into acting out sexually."

"It is so hard to remain pure in the midst of this overwhelming onslaught of sex marketing."

Some students went so far as to decry the current mode of dating. "We should cut out empty flirting and wasteful dating. Dating isn't a form of entertainment!" Others remarked that at some of the colleges they attend, dating and marriage have become too great of a focus.

In further discussion about sexuality, students were sharply critical of the church for its traditionally passive engagement of the issue with its young people. Most students focused on the failure of their local churches and local church leadership (i.e., pastors, Sunday School teachers, youth leaders) to adequately and maturely address the topic of sex in meaningful conversations with them. Several noted that the topic is considered taboo and is never discussed with them. Others expressly asked that parents and adults within the Body of Christ openly converse with them about sex—which includes discussing the challenges of abstinence in a postmodern culture and the boundaries and attributes of healthy relationships in a Christian context. The lengthy quote that follows is a stellar representation of the thoughts expressed by students regarding the failure of their parents and church leaders to discuss sex in a Christian context:

"Christian purity means that the church steps up and stops being so weird about sex. We need some conversation. We need it to be more than someone just saying 'don't do it.'

"Even parents need to step up. I never had a conversation with my parents that went straight to the point. Just tell me about putting God first and having self-control, not just with sex, but with all aspects of my life.

"What's perceived in the media is not what sex is. You don't just have sex with someone, leave the next morning, and carry on with life. I just got married and found there is so much that nobody tells you. There's stuff that's not talked about; it's just hidden.

"The problem is that if you don't talk about it, then you just get more and more curious. The more you think about something you're told not to do, the more you become curious.

The counter-effect is to talk about it. The truth should be discussed, as well as steps toward pursuing God, rather than the command to stay away from sex."

At one table, among the seven students present, only one had had a meaningful conversation about sex within the Christian lifestyle with a parent or church leader. But even so, the participants were unanimous as they begged for conversations and new attitudes about this subject.

"The church needs to have an open discussion where guilt, blame, and shame are not placed. I need to be able to ask questions openly for growth. Otherwise, sex is always seen as 'dirty and bad.' Basically, we need to talk about it."

Rob Bell's book *Sex God* is a great resource that forthrightly brings the discussion of sexuality out into the open where it belongs, without embarrassment or shame. He looks at the issue with a fresh lens—and an ancient one as well—turning back to the New Testament concept of *agape* love to evaluate relationships. In his book he states, "Sex is not the search for something that's missing. It's the expression of something that's been found. It's designed to be the overflow, the culmination of something that a man and a woman have found in each other."[13]

The young adults represented in these conversations obviously desired a deeper connection with mentors within the community of Christ who would come alongside them and engage them in relationships that would lead to a meaningful and ongoing dialogue about sex, dating, and purity. But this was only the beginning of their desire to experience purity within the larger faith community rather than looking at it solely from a self-centered perspective. Many students hold the desire to live pure lives as part of a dynamic community that would encourage and affirm their efforts.

"Purity is about community."

"We need to tell each other what to avoid."

"We try to live in *light* of God's story and to find our place *in* God's story—all within a community."

"Pastors and youth pastors alone cannot make these connections. There is a lack of significant, real relationships."

Millennial students are reaching out to the church as a whole, crying for relationships that will allow them to learn and grow and mature within the faith community. The desire evidenced in these discussions is not solely for same-age relationships, either. Students long for relationships with older adults as well as with younger members of their congregations. They call for the removal of age divisions and the establishment of a more family-oriented community where they may belong, follow, and lead.

The idea of working out purity within the faith community became an even more important concept in the discussions of how we as Christians live out that purity in the world, in our day-to-day decisions about where to go and what to do. How do we determine what is evil and what is not? Should Christians limit the kinds of establishments they visit in order to maintain their faith? What qualifies as a legitimate opportunity for witness? The importance and necessity of strong relationships within the community, and the input of a mentor who would help negotiate how purity is worked out in everyday life, has become absolutely clear.

The choices and moral dilemmas we face regarding purity are nothing new, and we have many resources in the twenty-first century that allow us to sharpen one another, to come alongside one another, and to grow in the grace and knowledge of our Lord Jesus Christ.

Students enunciated the importance of other, often less-discussed issues within the lifestyle topic. These issues were identified as behaviors that were also harmful to the Christian witness. One student remarked that "our lifestyle should be distinctly Christian," a lifestyle that does not include complaining, bad attitudes, hypocrisy, or the exploitation of others—all traits that are very often found in Christians.

One of the most heartening themes to emerge from this discussion on lifestyle was the importance of broadcasting the Christian lifestyle through the expression of love and acceptance to any and all. Student after student noted the essence of living Christlike as one who loves and serves others. The concept of servanthood emerged continually in the discussions of purity and lifestyle—convincing evidence that these twentysomethings strive not only to be mentored within the faith community, but also to take their places as servants reaching others outside of that community.

> **"Empathy: authenticate through servanthood. Love is agape—it is to love, expecting nothing in return."**

> **"Avoid the attitude of superiority; instead, choose servanthood."**

The challenge of this chapter, and of this discussion, however, is to the organized church, an institution young adults see as having frequently failed to engage them in meaningful models of purity. They see the current church as being afraid to even define the concept. And their critique is stinging.

> **"The church is afraid to define purity."**

> **"The church has sheltered itself from the real world."**

> "We need good resources and good teachers for Sunday School that will teach the message of Christ instead of behaviors that we shouldn't do."

> "We have poor teachers who are not prepared to teach lifestyle foundations rather than external behaviors."

While this critique is sharp, the desire of the millennials is obvious as well: to be part of the solution. They want to be part of the faith community that grows up, addresses the issues it has not faced, and moves forward in faith together.

## Lifestyle Discipleship
By David Kyncl

A few years ago, you could find just about every product imaginable inscribed with the letters "W.W.J.D."—What Would Jesus Do?

While some may consider the phrase cliché, it is a question that I find myself considering on a regular basis, particularly in light of the responses given and questions raised in this chapter.

God began to transform me as a student at the University of Kansas in the early 1980s. I was discipled by Gary Gilles through the ministry of Campus Crusade for Christ. For the first time in my life, I realized that God's Word applied to me. He not only created me, He loves me, and He forgives me.

Obedience in my faith began through this mentoring relationship as I was challenged to accept His love and forgiveness, and to acknowledge that I was a part of His creation. It was in this setting that I began to realize that the Great Commission was to obey *all* that God commanded.

As a result of this two-year investment in Campus Crusade for Christ, I realized that God wanted me to love Him with all my heart and to love others as I loved myself. And I realized that He wanted me to make disciples, just as Gary Gilles had done with me.

Since that time, I have had the opportunity to serve on a number of campuses. In each setting, God has allowed me to invest in the lives of college-aged young men and to disciple them to become more like Him.

At the 2:8 House, which is our campus ministry at the University of Oklahoma, students are invited into our home to share a meal with us each week. Four students live in apartments on the second floor of our home. They are a part of our family. For some students, this may be their first exposure to a home where both the mother and father are present. It may be the first time they experience a family in which both parents are Christian. Whatever their prior experiences, our home is a place where they can see our faith at work throughout our daily lives. It is a place where they are safe to ask tough questions about how our lives fit into God's plan.

God also continues to teach and challenge me through the many conversations with these twentysomethings. Many of the topics discussed in this chapter are topics that have been raised around the dining room table or in the living room of the 2:8 House. For example, when discussing purity, one student stated, "the church is afraid to define purity." We are quick to discuss the importance of sexual purity, especially as it applies to life before marriage. We even discuss how Christ drew the line at lusting after another person. But yet, we seem to never *define* purity. How does sexual purity apply to those of us who are married? Is it possible that Christ is also concerned about purity in other areas of our lives?

Our speech?

Our attitudes?

Our appetites?

Our thoughts?

If so, how do we, as a community, love one another in a way that reflects purity in these areas?

Another topic that has been discussed in our living room is wealth. We realize that many of us in the United States have been blessed with wealth. Compared to those in developing countries, one could argue that we are all wealthy. Is God concerned about how we spend our money, our time, or our talents? Would Jesus drive a luxury or sports car? Would He spend five dollars on a cup of coffee, even if it was a latte? Is Christ concerned about the size of our house payment? Is a tithe of our first fruits still a relevant guideline? What about the rich young ruler who was asked to sell *all* that he had and give it to the poor?

We have also been challenged by the students we know to more carefully consider the environment. A couple of years ago, a few students asked us about the amount of disposable dishes we used during our free lunch each week. Would we be better stewards of the environment if we stopped using so much Styrofoam? It was easy to answer yes, but it was a little more difficult to imagine keeping up with the dishes for a hundred students. A few friends from our local church volunteered to help us do just that. Their willingness to help us allowed them to meet the students and develop friendships with them. The 2:8 House's testimony has been strengthened as we have been willing to consider the environmental impact of our decisions.

So what does a distinctly Christian lifestyle look like? As questions like these continue, we encourage students to remember that there is one place to turn for guidance—His Holy Word. And as the author of Colossians reminds:

So, chosen by God for this new life of love, dress in the wardrobe God picked out for you: compassion, kindness, humility, quiet strength, discipline. Be even-tempered, content with second place, quick to forgive an offense. Forgive as quickly and completely as the Master forgave you. And regardless of what else you put on, wear love. It's your basic, all-purpose garment. Never be without it. Let the peace of Christ keep you in tune with each other, in step with each other. None of this going off and doing your own thing. And cultivate thankfulness. Let the Word of Christ—the Message—have the run of the house. Give it plenty of room in your lives. Instruct and direct one another using good common sense. And sing, sing your hearts out to God! Let every detail in your lives—words, actions, whatever—be done in the name of the Master, Jesus, thanking God the Father every step of the way *(3:12-17, TM)*.

## Food for Thought

While the church may do well at pointing out lifestyle issues that are contrary to its core beliefs, how is the church helping its people understand the reasons behind its contrary stance? How is the church displaying love to those who are living questionable lifestyles? Is the church truly loving them and assisting them in healing? Or is the church simply preaching at them and creating deep feelings of guilt, yet not providing any solutions for change? Today's pluralistic culture teams with lifestyles and practices that do not align with the Christian perspective. What is the church's response to this? According to the twentysomethings in our discussion groups, the church has done a significantly poor job of teaching purity in life and in sexuality. If there is to be positive change in this area, what must the church do to make that change?

# Chapter 3
# Ministry and Calling

## Insights on Ministry and Calling
From Liz Perry

*Liz Perry reclines in the chair behind her desk, breathing a sigh of relief and exhaustion that the week is finally over. An admissions counselor at Trevecca Nazarene University, she has just completed a long week of teen camp at the TNU campus. She brushes her hair back over her shoulder, straightens a few papers on her already pristine desk, and then smiles at me.*

*She is ready.*

*I have known Liz since she was a teenager in my youth group. I have seen her passion for Christ develop over the years as she's grown into adulthood, and I'm proud of the young, professional woman of God she has become. She is brilliant and purposeful in all that she does. And when the opportunity arose to interview a person on the call to ministry, I didn't debate long on whom I wanted to talk to.*

*Liz brushes an errant strand of hair from her face and steeples her hands in front of her. After a moment of idle chitchat, we begin.*

*"Liz, when I say 'the church' and 'calling people to ministry,' what comes to mind for you?" I ask. "What is your impression of the church's effort to call people into its ministry?"*

Liz hesitates for a moment, her forehead wrinkled in deep thought. Then she says, "Well, there are many different kinds of ministry. There's ministry that is local and ministry that is abroad. We tend to lump missions into ministry that is abroad, and we have no problems motivating people to go on a mission trip, which is an incredible thing. However, many people neglect the local ministry that's happening in the areas around them. We will literally move our churches and congregations to the suburbs, or to safe, nice areas where we can package a clean deal. Meanwhile, we've got urban areas that are hurting economically, spiritually, and socially. We tend to stay away from that because we think it's not a seeker-friendly environment."

I find it intriguing that she moves directly to such a deep subject, rather than slowly warming into the issue. I press for more. "Why do you think that is? You say it's not seeker-friendly. Are there deeper reasons why the church isn't doing a good job of calling people into what you've defined as local ministry?"

"I think our culture sees it as more fashionable and that it requires less investment to send people abroad," she responds. "That's because you don't even have to do the work. Take short-term missions trips. You spend a couple of weeks meeting people and doing good deeds, and then you come back to your safe neighborhood and your family. You never have to see those people again.

"Local ministry is about interpersonal relationships, relationships that are supposed to continue growing and continue throughout life. Those kinds of relationships must be fostered over time. But time, unfortunately, is not something that is invested in a whole lot."

"OK, let's switch gears," I say, wanting to come at this from another angle. "You went to Olivet Nazarene University and knew people who were called into full-time ministry—be that pastoral ministry, youth ministry, worship ministry, or whatever form that takes. How good of a job is the church doing in calling people into professional ministry positions?"

Liz jumps right in without hesitating on her response. "That's a great question. In college, I was surrounded by a group of older guys and girls who were theology majors. I had the pleasure of watching them walk through their higher education. Many started out wanting to be pastors, but by the end of it, a majority of them graduated with their theology major and had decided to do something other than full-time ministry."

"Really?"

"Yes. A lot of them were jaded about the church from things that they had seen or that they had learned about. They no longer wanted to be professional ministers. Instead, a lot of them have gravitated toward more grass roots stuff. Some have opened coffee shops. Others have started doing music on the side or what have you," she explains, as she brushes the stray hair out of her face again.

"Well, what do you think that says about the church's ability to call people into professional ministry?" I ask.

"I think it says, perhaps, that the church is calling with its voice, but maybe not calling into ministry itself," Liz answers leaning forward onto her elbows, driving the point home. "People sense authenticity. They move towards what they know to be real. If they find that the church—in its current state—is unappealing, and that pastors, mentors, and leaders aren't being the gospel, then they're going to be disheartened. They try to find a way out before they become that way themselves."

"So what about the church calling the laity into ministry?"

She thinks a moment. "I sure have seen a lot of altar calls about it. There are a lot of opportunities for people to come forward and answer the call. But unfortunately, the church brings the call into ministry down to a very small level. The church makes people think that being in ministry means you have to be a pastor or a youth pastor.

"That thinking doesn't leave a lot of creativity. Perhaps a layperson wants to work in the social justice scene. Or perhaps Christian counseling, or different things like that. Unfortunately, there just aren't many outlets for that kind of ministry. If we were just more creative about showing people what ministry in itself can look like, more people would be drawn into it.

"I'm involved in the Church of the Nazarene. And I think we do a pretty decent job of calling the laity into ministry, but it's obviously not enough. There are still so many hurts and needs around us that aren't being met in local communities."

Liz leans back in her chair again, brushing the stubborn tuft of hair from her face one more time. "I think that the call to being involved in ministry becomes a self-centered ministry. It's like the self-help books that offer ways to perfect your Christian faith. But once people feel 'perfected,' they don't see the need to extend. Well, the gospel clearly states that we will overflow onto others. Once you are filled up, it can only come outward. So, though they are working on their own faith, somehow it only goes so far and there just is very little extension out into the community."

"Because we have so many professional ministers nowadays, do you think there's more of a feeling from the laity that says, 'Well we're paying them to do the work so we just don't have to worry about it'?" I ask her.

She nods agreement. "Yeah! I mean it feels really great to put your check into the offering plate. You can go home with a clean conscience because you gave at church. However, that's not transformational in lives. People have to be transformed by the interaction they have with others."

"So you're saying that involvement in ministry, in and of itself, is a transformational act?"

"Yes. Exactly," Liz responds. "Ministry involves interacting with others. It's this interrelational thing that God has called us into. That's the kingdom of heaven. And I don't really think that we're there yet."

"So what you're saying is that the church is not showing the transformational work of being involved in ministry and the benefits therein. True?"

She swivels in her chair and grabs a pen from the desk. "Yeah. Let's say we're on a continuum." With the blunt end of the pen, she draws an imaginary line across her desk and points at one end of the line. "The church is on one side and on the other side of the continuum is secular society. We think that it has to be appealing for them in order for them to come more towards our side. So we make everything very clean. You know, throw VBS once a year and then you don't really have to worry about the kids of the community any longer because it's very clean and safe and you've got your two hours a night that you give. We think that will actually draw people in—being safe and clean and not getting our hands dirty.

"But that's absolutely the opposite of what Christ did. When we see where people are suffering in the world, it's as if we see more of a release of the power of God there. It's in the places where you're not allowed to be in a church, the underground communities—that's actually where the church is thriving."

The level to which she has thought through this subject impresses me. "If you were to give advice to the church on what they need to do to call people into ministry, what would you say?"

Again, no hesitation in her response. "The church needs to take it back to the Gospels, back to what we know about Jesus Christ. Because if He was God incarnate and He was doing things that changed the world, then we need to look at those acts and replicate them. Christ was countercultural. So I say the church needs to also be countercultural."

*"And the culture says what?"*

*"Watch out for yourself."*

*"And you say to be countercultural means . . .?"*

*"To watch out for others at the cost of yourself."*

## Roundtable Discussion Overview

In his book *The Call*, Os Guinness defines this oft-discussed concept: "What do I mean by 'calling'? For the moment let me say simply that calling is the truth that God calls us to himself so decisively that everything we are, everything we do, and everything we have is invested with a special devotion and dynamism lived out as a response to his summons and service."[14] Students seemed to embrace this encompassing definition, which serves as a summons initiated with Christ's desire that every human come to know Him personally—that we each come to understand how complete and total His love is for us.

As we grow in the knowledge of who God is and how completely He loves us, how He created us and equipped us and commissioned us, Christ challenges us to love God and to love and disciple others. We are called to love God with all our mind, soul, heart, and strength. We are called to love others. We are called to disciple others and to train and encourage those disciples to disciple others.

With that in mind, we proposed three main questions for this discussion.

- **Describe your understanding of calling.**

- **How do you plan to live out your ministry or your calling?**

- **What does it mean to be missional?**

As the discussions unfolded, several common themes emerged. One primary theme was that a calling is at the same time universal and personal, and relational and vocational. Calling may come at one particular moment, but it continues throughout a lifetime. It is not just the destination, but also the journey. Everyone is called, and everyone is challenged to respond in obedience to God.

In this respect, students returned repeatedly to the idea that calling is universal. Not only are we each called into relationship with Him, we are each called into relationship with other people around us.

"First we are called to be part of His family."

"Everyone has a role in the Kingdom."

"We need to build stronger bonds between us and God, our children and God, the church and God. We need to become true followers of Christ, becoming Christians through personal relationships with Him."

This call is encompassed and defined through relationships—our individual relationship with Jesus Christ and our relationships with one another as we live out our calling in community.

"I know Him and know His direction for me through a close personal relationship of prayer."

"For our generation, it is imperative to have a personal relationship with Christ. Our generation needs mentorship and discipleship; until we get those, we are lost, even as Christians."

One student introduced a profound concept: the idea of being lost, even as a part of the Body of Christ. It is essential that a close, intimate relationship with Christ becomes a defining characteristic of those in our local congregations. That ongoing relationship will then equip each member to intentionally invest into the lives of others— what is often called discipleship. Related to this issue, in Steve Shadrach's book *The Fuel and the Flame*, he makes this statement: "If we love someone we will pray for them, share the gospel with them, and lay our lives down for them. Our motive in ministry has to be our genuine, authentic love for others, and the Great Commission should flow out of the Great Commandment."[15] Twentysomethings desire such love. (Don't we all?) If met with such compassion, they certainly seem to be ready to return it!

"Sometimes I wish I had picked a different major and then just added the ministry as an outlet, like being a teacher and going somewhere to teach English. We need to be educated in many different areas so we can understand other people's experiences and minister in practical, meaningful ways."

"I'm majoring in Christian ministries. But how serious is someone going to take me as a pastor? If I had something else to offer and could build relationships, how much more meaningful would that be? I could minister through other venues and then add the discipleship."

"In our churches, we focus on ministry staff. Therefore the laity sit back and get lazy. Laypeople need to be developed and need to disciple people so that they in turn can disciple people, and so on."

In this context, these students highlighted the glaring distinction made by the church of those called into full-time Christian service, which is usually thought to mean we serve Him as a pastor or teacher in the church. While God does equip and call some individuals to fulfill specific roles within the church, He also calls others to specific roles within society at large. In either case, our call is to love, to minister, to serve, and He equips us for each role. The twentysomethings at the M7 conference recognized the disconnect between full-time Christian service and other careers. And their critique of this dichotomy is apparent.

"Calling is not bound by traditional church structure. It is not, 'Go out into all the church,' but 'Go out into all the world.'"

"God's call is where our deepest gladness meets the world's deepest hunger."

"People don't have to be pastors to have a calling."

While some may find their place of service within the church, each of us is called to love our neighbors, and disciple and serve others. God's call requires a response from each of us—to follow His leadership in our lives through walking daily in obedience. One student said it best: "I'm still not positive on the specifics of my call—but I know that obedience is key. It is a step-by-step process, a service to our community and church." Our understanding becomes more complete as we daily walk in faith and obediently respond to His Word and work through us.

We often hear the Great Commission with the emphasis to *go* and make disciples. However the call is actually *as we are going* to make disciples. We begin where we are today, in our church and community. As we are going, He continues to guide, direct, equip, and bless our efforts. One student commented, "We mistake it to mean that we are to go somewhere else in the world and do missions. That's part of it, but it also means being involved in your own community."

> "To be missional is to realize what and where the heart of God is, and then sacrificing yourself for others in those ways and in those places."
>
> "It is a lifestyle of living for God, loving people around me, and building connections to share Christ."

As the Holy Spirit makes us aware of the needs of others around us, our success should be measured by our response to His leadership. As we are faithful in our response to Christ, we fulfill our call.

One participant wrapped up the discussion on missional calling quite profoundly by saying, "Be bold: Luther used a nail for his thesis, not a band-aid."

## Ministry and Calling Testimonial
By Rhonda Dean Kyncl

The principle issue that surfaces in any discussion of ministry and calling is the church's continual support of the erroneous division of *vocational calling* and *secular career*. This false dichotomy is perpetuated when the church reserves its highest accolades and greatest resources for the men and women called into the vocational ministries of pastor and missionary, and consequently snubs the student who settles for a career in accounting or some other secular field. Os Guinness's book *The Call* describes two particular forms of the church's wayward portrayal of calling. The first is the Catholic distortion where the clergy is elevated above everyone else because the clerical life is superior to the menial nature of other work. The second is the Protestant distortion where work replaces the spiritual sense of vocation and ignores the spiritual aspects of any and all calling. Guinness goes on to explain that we all have a *primary calling* to serve and worship God the Creator. Then, we've each been given a *secondary calling*, what we now refer to as our vocation. None of these vocations is greater than any other.[16]

I lived under this false division when I left college. Growing up in the church as the daughter of a full-time pastor, I wanted nothing to do with vocational ministry. I had my heart set on earning a liberal arts degree and living an independent life that did not involve anyone being able to interrupt my vacations by dying or getting married. I achieved this goal and settled into a nine-to-five job—but it didn't give me any spiritual satisfaction. I got exactly the life I wanted, but found it increasingly unfulfilling.

Thankfully during this time, God led me to a Bible study called *Experiencing God* that was being offered at my church. This study proved to be a benchmark for my sense of calling. My husband also helped a great deal. He was a layman, serving at a secular university, who consistently invested his time in mentoring young men on campus. He was not a full-time minister according to the church's definition, but he was absolutely engaged in full-time ministry through his work of discipleship on campus.

Gradually, and as a natural part of our spiritual lives, God led both my husband and me to a deeper sense of what He wanted to do with our lives. He led us to a call that included all of our past experiences as well as some healthy faith for what He could do through us in the future. We pursued the call together and ended up as campus ministers (where we still serve) at the University of Oklahoma (OU). While on the OU campus, I've also worked toward my Ph.D. and now teach English Composition to first-year students. My calling encompasses my entire life, but it is not at all what an evangelical would look at as a vocational call. I now realize God's intention for my life all along and it consumes my entire sphere of responsibility.

My call is lived out on a daily basis as I meet with two classes of students (usually thirty-five to forty students each). I pray for them nightly and ask God to direct our semester and our studies. I invite them over to our home for lunch or dinner at least a couple of times during the semester and to our campus-wide free lunch held every Tuesday. My goal is to build a relationship with them. I don't do much, if any, verbal evangelism—my outreach is living a life that stands out in its contrast to the academics and students I rub elbows with every-day. My calling encompasses not only my work with my husband as a campus minister, but also my teaching, my parenting, my role in our church, my studying, and my relationships with any and all with whom I come in contact.

While I have come to terms with what I believe is a deeper sense of spiritual calling, there is still the challenge of the *church's* response to the notion of calling. I am often questioned by individuals within the church who think that I need to be ordained if I really want to minister. I cringe when pastors glowingly announce that so-and-so, a student a' a nearby Christian college, has made a decision to pursue full-time ministry, when sitting next to me is a student at our secular university who has decided to pursue full-time ministry as well—as an engineer or a psychologist or an accountant. Yet no one makes a big deal about that.

So what must the response be? We must mentor leaders who will be missionaries within corporations and militaries and political systems and other institutions all over the world. If we confine our idea of calling to pastors, missionaries, and evangelists, we are already irrelevant to the twenty-first-century world.

There is no secular versus sacred. God does not value one vocation over any other; He is the Caller, and He skillfully positions each of us in the places where our lives are needed as His salt and light. There is only God's work done in all places and at all times by those He has called. Failing to critique the dichotomy of vocational ministry versus lay ministry will not only make us irrelevant to the world, eventually it will erode the essence of our message within our community as well. Promoting vocational ministers to the neglect of those called into other full-time areas of ministry alienates the majority of our congregations who work outside the walls of the institutionalized church —those who work in, ironically, the exact places Jesus called us to go with the message of His Good News.

## Food for Thought

The calling that God places on the lives of His people is sacred, no matter how big or small that calling may be. However, has the church gone far enough in helping its people recognize that they are called by God to participate in the ministry of the Body? Has the church celebrated the calling of the laity as much as it celebrates the calling of its full-time ministers? Or, has the church so divided the two types of callings that it has minimized the importance of the calling of the laity—to the point that such a calling is no longer important to the Kingdom? If so, what changes must the church make to rectify this position?

# Chapter 4
# Church and Community

## Insights on Church and Community
From Phil Burkhart

*Phil walks into my office and sits in the guest seat. His infectious smile fills my office with his presence. The plate glass window behind him frames him perfectly, the light casting a glow around him like a massive halo. Phil is a brilliant, young worship pastor whose responsibilities in his congregation stretch far beyond that of the typical worship pastor.*

*As I clear some of my paperwork out of his way, we chat amicably. I sense a depth in him, a kindred soul. I like him immediately.*

*"So, Phil," I begin, "tell me your thoughts on the church and community."*

*"Community? As in the church community? Or the local community that the church resides in?" he asks.*

*"Maybe both," I respond, "but specifically, I want to know your thoughts on the church and its involvement in the local community."*

*Phil doesn't take much time to think. "The church isn't involved in the community as much as it should be. Some denominations do a better job of this than others, but the Church of the Nazarene on the whole seriously lacks in its participation in the local community.*

"We should be intricately involved in the community. Our congregations have facilities that need to be used, and not just for the church body. A church's facilities should be viewed as an extension of the community, as a part of the community. If we aren't offering to the community what we have for their use, then we are missing part of our purpose.

"We've got meeting rooms that shouldn't be reserved just for Sunday School or church meetings. Why aren't we making those rooms available to the community for their use whenever they need them? Boy Scouts, Girl Scouts, baseball, basketball—all different types of organizations can always use empty rooms. Why doesn't this happen?"

I consider his words for a moment and then ask, "What about organizations that stand for things contrary to what we believe? Such as planned parenthood groups, or the gay activists?"

"Well, OK, there are probably some limits. We probably shouldn't be seemingly supportive of practices that are contrary to who we are as a people. After all, it is about being a positive light in the community."

"Then what are we doing wrong?"

"What are we doing wrong?" he repeats, thinking through his response. "We're called to relationships with people. We expect people to come be a part of us, rather than us going to them. Expecting them to come to us pulls us out of being involved in the community. Church shouldn't be a separatist organization, but we've made it that, haven't we? We need to focus on being out in the community, on going to them rather than having them come to us. That's how Jesus operated. He went to where the people were. He didn't expect them to come to Him. It's not about a holy huddle within the church walls; it's about huddling within the community."

"What do you mean by that last statement?"

Phil repositions himself in his chair. "What I mean is that the church has gone all wrong. It has moved to existing for itself rather than existing for the salvation of the world, or even for its individual communities. We think the only way we can reach people is to bring them through the doors of the church. Yet there are a lot of people who may never come to church and we've got to find a way to connect to them. Maybe it's by making the church facilities available for their use. Or maybe it's more purposeful, like through small group ministry. We should encourage people just to come to small groups, and who cares if they come to an actual church service."

He pauses for a moment, and then continues. "You know, society views the church as a bunch of pointless hypocrites, as having nothing to do with individual lives. Sadly, the unchurched part of society doesn't see the church as any different than themselves.

"And even in the church, people turn it into something about themselves. Church has become self-serving to many. But it's not about them and what they want to do. It's about what God is calling them to do, no matter what.

"The perspective of the world is 'Why would people give to the church?' They don't see the church as being able to make a difference. That's the saddest part of the whole issue. As followers of Christ, we haven't done our job of setting an example. We were once people just like them; however, Christ has transformed us and we are continually being transformed. Yet they don't see the church as being different, so why would they make a change."

His words are profound and deeply felt as they settle in on me. He is a young man wise beyond his years.

## Roundtable Discussion Overview

The spiritual health and vigor of the local church is essential as it represents Christ to others. In the Great Commission, Jesus set the model to begin in Jerusalem and then continue to Judea, to Samaria, and to the ends of the earth. In other words, begin locally and spread out from there to the whole world. With that in mind, the health of the local congregation is critical to the health of the global church.

The local church is the one area where the students at the M7 conference have the most experience. This is evidenced by the depth and passion this particular discussion generated. While the characteristics and demographics of local churches vary greatly, similar perspectives emerged.

The initial questions which began this discussion included:

- **What is the role of the local church in your life?**
- **What do you see as your role in the life of the local church?**
- **What are the things you think the church is very concerned about that it shouldn't be?**
- **What is most effective way to introduce your age-group to Jesus?**
- **What are you doing to address social issues in your city?**
- **Does the church have the authority to tell you anything?**
- **Does the church have authority?**
- **How should we respond to leaders in the church?**

While many students acknowledged that the local church has a place of authority in their lives, there were several students who cautioned that that authority was conditional.

"It's the church's job to speak authoritatively."

"Church itself has no authority; it only has authority if it is doing God's will."

"Church has authority regardless. You go to church because you want to. God places people in authority in the church. But, we should always evaluate what they say."

"We need to respect the church but we shouldn't always just accept it without processing."

"Does the church have authority? It depends on how and what we are asked to do."

In the discussion of the church's authority, the role of accountability as it relates to authority became a topic of interest.

"The church's authority is weakened if the membership does not hold people accountable to the standards."

"Leaders of the church need to be accountable. They should be more honest with their congregation as to what they are going through."

During these discussions it also became clear that the local church plays a significant role in the lives of many of these students. Several rejoiced in the significant impact experienced through the local church. Others felt distant and disconnected.

"Church is a great part of my life even as a college student. I couldn't make it without church. I need the relationships."

"My church is my family; I could not be here without that family."

"The church is mentoring me and providing a place of connection."

"I couldn't be a good Christian apart from church."

"I don't feel I have a role as a college student. I feel void in college."

"Yes, church is extremely important to the Body as a whole. It is the hub, even though it may not always be correct."

"The local church provides guidance. It feeds my soul and provides time away from a busy week. The local church allows me to become part of something bigger than myself."

Several common themes opened up from the conversations as students shared their concerns about the local church. They were asked to identify areas of focus within the church that should not be emphasized, as well as areas that did not receive enough attention. In response, several students discussed the lack of community within their local churches as evidenced by the lack of intergenerational interaction within the church body.

> "The lack of community sends a message to those in and outside the church."
>
> "The different generations should be able to work together in that rich heritage."
>
> "The forty-plus age-group is afraid of changes made to help reach this generation."
>
> "The separation of ages, lack of interaction, and lack of knowledge are barriers."
>
> "I wish the church would support me. I also wish that the younger generation would be emotionally supported and that the older generation would believe in us."
>
> "It seems like the younger people don't matter."
>
> "Community has to play a central role. Who doesn't want to be loved?"

Another focus that students felt their local fellowships overemphasized was the attention paid to the numbers, particularly in the areas of attendance, buildings, and cash. Overwhelmingly, students decried this tendency to spotlight these quantitative measures that ultimately may distract from the human side of Kingdom building.

> "Numbers are *an* indicator but not *the* indicator."

"I see castle building instead of Kingdom building."

"We focus on numbers rather than strengthening and developing the people already there."

"Monies raised should first go toward people, not buildings. Buildings should come from abundance."

"Reporting numbers seems unnecessary. Why is it significant that a thousand people go to our church or youth event?"

"What are we measuring? Bodies or fruit?"

"We don't need a $4 million building to have church."

Closely related to the misappropriation of time and energy put into castle versus Kingdom building is the lack of focus on more central human issues, such as social concerns. Students again voiced a poignant desire to see people affected by the outreach born through personal relationships, rather than being counted as just a number in the attendance.

"What are we doing about social issues? We should keep talking about them and keep them in front of us."

"Awareness—we need to become aware of opportunities where we can help. It is hard to be involved in big social issues. We should look for the small ways. Be faithful and God will provide ways to help out."

"Social issues are a huge part of this generation. We are aware of issues and want to work to fix them."

"We forget about service for the sake of service—a no strings-attached mind-set."

"The church is in a box. It is not looking beyond that box."

"We must be careful of drawing lines where we can and cannot go. Those hurt Christlike motives and ministry."

The responses to the questions surrounding discipleship were overwhelming. Unfortunately, for the sake of space allotted in this book we have been forced to significantly pare down the body of responses. The concerns of the twentysomethings centered on the lack of authentic discipleship that students have witnessed within their local churches.

"New believers need to be taught at the level of a child, i.e., a Bible with children's stories. They haven't learned it yet!"

"Discipleship is key. The older should always be mentoring the younger."

"The third part of the Great Commission is always left out! We've got to be going out into the world and baptizing, but we always forget the discipleship part. We aren't being taught the Word in this format or continuing to read our Bibles and learning and following Christ."

"There's too much focus on people leaving; it's time to focus on those staying."

Not only did students see a need for one-on-one discipleship relationships, they felt this need was especially significant for members of their own generation who remain looking in on the faith community from the outside. In discussing how to reach their peers, several students referred to Brian McLaren's book, *More Ready Than You Realize*. This book follows an e-mail dialogue that illustrates a spiritual friendship between McLaren and a college student named Alice. In his book, McLaren states, "Christian spiritual friendship is always about encouragement, empowerment, believing in people, whether we do so from 'up ahead' as mentors, from beside as peers, or even 'from behind' as students ourselves. It is not a matter of status at all. How could it be otherwise, considering Jesus, who washed his disciples' feet, took the role of a servant, and told his disciples they would do greater things than He did?"[17] The motivation of authentic friendship resonates with many of the students' comments.

"The deeper relationships are needed. It's not about numbers; it's about relationships, friendships, examples. If they never become Christians, so what! It is important to know and love one another."

"The do's and don'ts turn people off."

"The art of personal evangelism is relational. Your influence from your own life will speak the message."

"It's easy to sell someone on a good restaurant or movie and get them to go check it out. But what about your church?"

"Sometimes the theological jargon we use is great because it makes outsiders curious, but often it's just confusing."

"Most effective is loving and building community—loving people until they see something different in your life."

"Christianity isn't about fussing and fighting and hypocrisy. We need to show that Christianity is about loving, caring, and being there for one another."

"Relationships should not hinge on accepting Christ or not. People are turned off by people with agendas. Become friends because you love them."

Whether it is reaching out to their generation or working to address social issues one person at a time, these students desire a church that has returned to the essentials of the gospel. We must love the Lord God with all our hearts, all our minds, and all our strength. We must love one another as ourselves. The church must be a place, as McClaren talks about, where people can belong *before* they believe.[18]

Finally, the discussions turned to the students' dissatisfaction with church as entertainment. Students clearly saw the move to incorporate technology as particularly disingenuous when it replaces authentic human touch and relationships.

> "People need to start focusing on Jesus, not the church programs or big-screen TVs. Stop trying to influence people based on material merchandise; just push Jesus and He will shine bright enough to bring people in."

> "Church is for learning about Christ, not providing entertainment. You may have more youth coming, but do they know Christ? They don't take church seriously. Are they willing to die for their faith? Generally, no."

> "Be careful that the message is not lost in changing methods."

The college and university students in our discussions repeatedly returned to the desire—or rather the demand—for a church that authentically welcomes them to the table. They long for relationships that hold significance and that persevere through all phases of their development and growth. They know that without such discipleship, their status as believers is tenuous at best. They need the Body of Christ; and obviously, the Body of Christ needs them. Without their energy and vigor, churches languish and lose touch with an entire generation. If church cannot offer discipleship through relationships as Christ exemplified, it will become irrelevant to this generation. These students are calling the church to revisit its decisions, programs, and methods by which the local church conducts life as a congregation.

## Church and Community

By Jon Middendorf

Having spent seventeen years now working with youth and young people, I am more convinced than ever that our younger generations are starving for Christian community.

Oklahoma City First Church of the Nazarene is nearing its hundredth birthday, and yet we are a congregation in transition, a transition nourished by the appetites and energies of our twentysomethings. We are blessed to be less than ten minutes from Southern Nazarene University, and because of this proximity, we have prioritized ministry to university students and young adults for many years. Our close attention given to the climate and culture of young people has given us a front-row seat to the changing nature of twentysomething faith.

The traditional worship experience in many of our churches happens on the platform where we have, in most cases, ample resources invested in spotlights, sound equipment, and technology. Participants in this kind of worship sit in the pews and take the posture of consumerism— taking in the "show" like they would at the neighborhood theater.

The platform is typically two to four steps above the level of the congregation. The words coming from that platform are coming *down* to the congregation from "on high." There is an implied—and at times explicit—sense of authority and superiority emanating from the stage.

There are several churches that have perfected the performance of the Sunday service, and some of those churches are seeing wave after wave of young people. Getting these folks to come and spectate is one thing; getting them to become part of the community is something completely different.

But there are those who recognize their need of just such relationships, people who are going to move around until (a) they find a home for friendship and faith, or (b) they become disenchanted and cynical, no longer believing that such a place can exist. The students around the tables at M7 seemed like this second group. They made a special effort to speak into the process—evidence of their hope that things can change and be different, evidence that they are looking for places to belong.

It's not the lights or the raised platform that will disappoint these young adults; rather, it's traditional morning worship without the daily and weekly relationships. The words sung and spoken from the stage may or may not have authority and credibility with young believers. The office of pastor or preacher no longer comes with an assumed sense of respect or reverence. With these twentysomethings, respect and credibility are earned virtues, earned *between* Sundays by the hard work of relationships. This earned respect, in turn, gives credence to the words sung and preached on a Sunday morning.

The pastor of twentysomethings can no longer afford the distance that used to exist between the platform and the people in the pews. A pastor has authority and credibility only to the extent that he or she is able to embody the dreams of the Kingdom and the points of the sermon. Now the twentysomethings are saying, "Preach and talk to me. Don't preach at me." Without these kinds of faith-forming relationships, not only is the credibility of the pastor in question, but the credibility of the entire church will be in question too. At this point the resources spent on the traditional worship experience will be evidence of mismanaged funds and misguided thinking. Twentysomethings will have already begun looking for the exits.

At OKC First Church, we are addressing the above in two ways. First, we have stayed close enough to an emerging culture to recognize the changing definitions and strategies surrounding concepts like credibility and authority. We are a fellowship organized to include our Sunday morning worship services, but those services are not the defining moments of our church. We are a busy bunch, working and meeting and praying together between Sundays at both our church and at various places around the city. The Sunday services are a reflection of our lives together throughout the week.

Second, we have begun another congregation underneath the umbrella of OKC First. *Kaleo,* a group of sixty to eighty people of various ages and places, meets and ministers during the week, and their Sunday worship gatherings are much less formal and much more conversational than the more traditional morning service. Coffee and questions are regular and vital elements of this casual and yet liturgical-minded body of believers.[19]

Another issue that seems prominent to this age-group is the separation of friendship from the church. To these believers, and many others of varying ages, friendship is both the means and the end of faith. While not relinquishing the idea of friendship with God, young believers are just as committed to the expression of faith known as friendship with others.

Twentysomethings demand that their churches teach, encourage, and demonstrate redemptive, generative friendships. Many traditional fellowships are recalibrating in order to maintain contact with generations of believers who are more reliant on friends and more open to varying definitions of family than ever before.

The Kaleo congregation's worship gatherings mirror the convictions practiced throughout the week. The sermons delivered are comfortable, casual, and conversational in nature, and the mobile nature of the room itself rehearses the mobile nature of a congregation ready and eager to participate in the redemption of the world. While I don't doubt the capacity of the morning congregation to be compassionate or redemptive, the Kaleo congregation, being smaller and more agile, moves quickly when given an opportunity to minister.

Kaleo spends next to nothing on the worship gatherings, opting instead to use their money to address both local and global needs. Recent offerings were collected to support Blood:Water Mission,[20] as well as the living expenses of a young mother in our fellowship. This format and mind-set is better equipped to connect with believers whose lives are so often marked by fluidity, activity, and friends.

No generation embodies, or at least longs to embody, that mind-set more than these twentysomethings. Theirs is an active faith, as we've mentioned before. But what's more, these young believers seem ready to take on the label of the Body of Christ, so long as they can participate, along with others, in the redemption of the world.

At Oklahoma City First, our young believers are bringing their imaginations to our calendar and budget meetings. We are listening to them as they bring opportunities for us to minister as the people of God, the Body of Christ. While many are forecasting the end of denominations, we are seeing loyalty and commitment from our young adults, provided they remain confident of our intentions to shape our budgets and ministries according to the mission of Christ.

With the input of our twentysomethings, we have overhauled the utilities and energy usage for our building. Automated thermostats and energy efficient lights are going to save money—money that can be spent helping and nurturing those around us.

Young believers are helping us to reimagine our communication strategies. Everything from our websites to our worship folders to our e-mail blasts are being shaped and edited by these technology-minded believers. They are making sure that our virtual presence is intentional and consistent with our Kingdom convictions.

The bad news is that our young believers are frustrated with the inability of the church to function as the Body of Christ. They see a mechanism more concerned with production than participation. They sense a lack of emphasis on relationship and friendship. They see an institution lacking the flexibility to move and respond quickly to issues on the local and global levels. And they are disenchanted with what they perceive to be a lack of vision and imagination that would allow the church to move in unison as Christ's Body.

The good news is that they haven't given up—not on their church and not on their dreams for what we can be and do. Let's continue to listen to one another, and let's give our students ownership and responsibility to lead us.

## Food for Thought

What is the church doing to transform community, or to be transformed by community in a positive way? Is the local congregation an offshoot of the community? Or is the community surrounding the local church a separate organization, functioning for its own purposes without regard for the community at large? Does the local church make its facilities available to the community, viewing its facilities as a tool to reach out to those in need? If not, then why not? How is the church viewed by the community? More poignantly, if the local congregation were to cease to exist, what effect would this have on its community? If none, what does that say about the effectiveness of that church within the location that it has been placed?

Chapter 5
# Church and Society

## Insights on Church and Society
From Jason Sivewright

*Another coffee shop, another conversation, another brilliant young adult. Jason sets his soy-peppermint latte squarely on the table in front of him before reclining in his chair. I cannot see his eyes through his mirrored sunglasses, but his wry smile and relaxed demeanor echo the confidence I have come to know in this young man.*

*I am encouraged to see Jason sitting across from me. There was a time when to have interviewed him in this setting would have been pointless. Although raised in the Church of the Nazarene from birth, his teenage years were marked with rebellion. But God's mercy sank its teeth into him a half-decade ago and his life has been transformed ever since. He is a trophy of God's immeasurable grace. And now, as a twenty-six-year-old man, he is heavily involved in the leadership of a church plant in the Kansas City area, and is the worship leader of that congregation. He is a brilliant writer, artist, and film director. And because of his connection with today's culture, I am craving his thoughts on the church as it relates to modern society.*

"So, Jason, how do you think society views the church in today's culture?" I ask.

He takes a long drink of his latte before responding. "Quite frankly, people outside of the church think we look pretty stupid. They wonder why we need all the different forms of Christianity. They wonder why we're not one unified church rather than a whole bunch of little churches. That's the question I get from my friends who aren't Christians. They want to know why I'm a Nazarene and not a Baptist. They want to know if I think Baptists are stupid or something. The answer, of course, is no, I don't think they're stupid. Society just doesn't understand the differences and it makes us look bad.

"As far as our society inside the church, I don't think the different denominations are a bad thing. People just have different ways of thinking. All in all, I just don't put much stock in how important those differences are against the bigger picture."

Strong words, but that is not unexpected from Jason. Although normally a quiet individual, if he knows you and is under the right circumstances, he is prone to speaking his opinion.

I push him for more. "What about your peers? Would they feel the same way?"

"I think we've just stopped believing that the differences are all that important. We just don't care about that stuff." He takes another sip of his coffee before continuing. "I'm a Nazarene because I grew up a Nazarene. But I don't condemn any other denomination at all. I was born and raised a Nazarene, and I have friends who were born and raised in other denominations, but we all have the exact same beliefs. So they just call themselves 'Followers of Jesus,' which is often considered nondenominational. It's the cool term now to be called nondenominational."

"Why is that the cool term?"

"I think it just goes along with everything, in that we are to accept everything. To say you're nondenominational means you're not bound to any church, you're just a follower of Christ."

"Do you think it has anything to do with pluralism?" I ask.

Jason nods his head, shrugs his shoulders, and says, "I think pluralism in the church, inside the realm that Jesus Christ is our Savior, is OK. There are just certain truths that are unmitigated. As in, you just can't change certain facts—God is God, and He sent His Son, Jesus. But beyond that, if it's inside that realm, then yeah, it's OK.

"It's those who have been in the church for a long time who hold fast to the rules of what we do or don't do as a denomination. Changing those rules or even starting a discussion about them isn't acceptable. But why not? Assuming you believe in the core values of Christianity, what denomination you are or what rules you go about to get there doesn't put you in the wrong."

His statement has sent my mind on a tangent that could use his opinion. "In the United States, the church has functioned as the moral center of our society for many years. Our constitution was founded on Judeo-Christian beliefs and our laws are drawn from that. Does church still play a role as the moral center of our society?"

"I guess so, but I really don't know if you can say there is a moral center to our society anymore. The church has kind of separated itself from the world so much that they just don't seem fit together. Morals and church go hand-in-hand, and people often lump those terms together, but I don't think the church has a strong enough influence on society to say that it really is the moral center."

"What is then?"

"Well, it's more like—morals? What is that word? We live in a world where my morals might not be your morals, and my truth is not your truth, but it's still true, you know? We live in a postmodern world where anything can be true if you believe it. And I can be sitting across from somebody who has a completely different set of truths, but I need to accept those truths just as much as I accept my own. That's just the world we live in." He pauses to catch a breath. "When you say morals, that's basically a term that doesn't mean anything. As bad as it is, it's like the Church of Scientology, in that we're all our own life forces. You know, we kind of go around and treat each other like that's OK. And it's just not rooted in anything. So the bad thing about it is that people will grasp onto any truth, and that's always, throughout history, been a scary thing for people to do."

"If that's the case, how does the church reach a society that doesn't have any set moral values? Or should the church even try to reach that society?" I ask.

"Well of course we definitely should. But what I look at as the greatest failure of my generation is that we've become so timid about our faith. We've become a group where being relevant is the main thing. And being relevant often means not saying the word Jesus or the word God. You don't say these things because that makes you ir-relevant to society. So in the process of doing that then we don't have the Good News anymore. So what we've done is we've made our message weak. We've come across as silent Christians. And that's terrible. That's why I think this generation coming up is so important, because I truly believe that God is instilling in them the power that we need. They're going to say 'I'm not going to be like the generation be-fore me, and be ashamed of what I know.' I mean, look at what we did. We gave the culture over to MTV. We gave the culture over to the Internet. And they did what they wanted with it, and now the minute we stand up and say Jesus, we're bigots. We've become so scared that we're weak and our message is weak. We might have become more relevant, but who cares? Nobody knows the message behind it."

*Jason's passion on this subject spills into his tone. It's obvious to me he's not just giving me nice words to make me feel good; his feelings on this are deep rooted.*

"So you're saying that the answer for the church—if we really want to become relevant again for society—is that we have to stand for something."

"Yeah. Put relevancy second to standing up for what you believe in and be willing to fight somebody for it. I don't mean physically, but say 'No! That's not right. There is truth, an absolute truth.' Or even, 'Your truth is not truth.' For years we've been afraid to confront people about how wrong they are. We just go around the fact. But that's got to change because people have just been led astray. I mean if you look at Scientology and how ridiculous it is, you wonder why people can be led into it—it's because they don't have anything else. Christians aren't saying 'No, this isn't truth.' We're not leading people to our truth. We're just being nice about things. But Scientologists are adamant about what they believe, and people will follow that."

"Doesn't that paint us as being intolerant?"

"No," he states flatly. "That's what we've been afraid of."

"We're afraid of being labeled intolerant?" I ask for clarification.

"Yeah. We're terrified of it, so we've been bashful. But Jesus was never like that. The key is you pick your battles. You stand on the core beliefs. It's just what we talked about regarding denominations. We don't fight the little stuff."

"What's little stuff?"

He takes another sip and then answers, "Well what about speaking in tongues? Who cares? I think it's really not that big of a deal unless it becomes a matter of having to speak in tongues in order for you to have a salvation experience. Then it's wrong. It's just wrong. We can't be nice about that. It's wrong. We just have to say that it's not truth, that it's outside of what Jesus taught and so the church just cannot accept tongues if that's what they're saying about it. Otherwise, who really cares?

"But getting back to society—society just sees the church as having to abide by a lot of rules. And they can't abide by those rules. They see it this way because we haven't done a good job of showing that Christianity is a fun life. The picture of church is a bunch of people sitting in pews, being bored. Just a bunch of rules of what you can't do. What we've done is we've made church a place of monotony and boredom and empty rituals. But that's not what Jesus wanted His Church to be. He wanted a place that was creative and filled with life. A place where people would be open and society would see that and want to be a part of it. But we don't. We get hung up on our crowd and keeping it our crowd and our way."

"What do you mean by 'our crowd and our way'?"

"Well, as an example, I went to play basketball at a friend's church the other day and I got kicked out because when some guy asked me if I attend the church, I said no. And because they had too many people to play, I got kicked out. Shouldn't it be the other way if we want to bring people in? Jesus would have turned the tables over on that guy. He made it about basketball, and it's not about that. It's about the community coming in to the church. That guy should have given up his spot so that I, an outsider, would feel welcomed. But we've become a closed society full of rules."

I check the time on my cell phone. I've got another appointment I'm backed up against. "So, any final thoughts on the church and society?" I ask.

"Well, it says in the Bible that the gates of hell will not be able to withstand the church. And it's true—throughout the years, the church has faced hard times. And while we might say bad things about the *church, don't say that it's dying. It will never die. We absolutely have to do all we can to improve the church and grow the church. But the Bible clearly says that Jesus will not let His Bride die."*

## Roundtable Discussion Overview

The church's role in society is much debated. The students at these round table discussions were no different than other believers who have diverse opinions and feelings about how the church should find its place in American society as a whole. The questions proposed during this time of discussion included:

- **Is denomination important?**
- **How do you feel about the American evangelical church and U.S. foreign policy?**
- **Describe the dynamics of the changing culture in and out of the church.**
- **What are a few ways you can impact the local and global church?**
- **How do you define tolerance?**
- **What is the church in twenty years?**

The first major discussion to occur within the context of the church and society focused on the segmenting of worshipers into specific denominations. The responses in this section must, of course, be considered in light of the fact that the discussions occurred during a denominationally-focused conference, and that most of the students maintain membership in that denomination. Nevertheless, the dialogue was interesting on several levels. Students did not reject their denominational ties, nor did they engage in an all-out critique of the denomination. In fact, many expressed a desire to see the denomination grow, change, and actively engage their culture. Many upheld the need for denominations to express their differences in beliefs and practices so that individuals may exercise their choices in places to worship and affiliations. A sample of these pro-denomination responses follows:

> "Denominations give us something small to connect to, they bring relationships."
>
> "Denominations provide opportunities for smaller congregations to do things on a bigger scale."
>
> "Denominations are great for resources, a belief system, and networking."
>
> "We tend to make it way too important, but it helps us to understand who we are."

Another significant part of this discussion went beyond the acceptance of denominational systems and toward a more pointed critique of the way denominations tend to become isolated from other groups —and therefore isolated from other views and influences.

> "The Church is the Bride. Eventually we will have to work together to be with Christ."
>
> "We don't have to always agree with everything, but we must support the collective decision as a member."

"We need to learn from Christians across denominational lines, as well as practicing community with others outside of our denomination."

"Denomination is about tradition. What's more
important is worshiping the same God."

Not surprisingly, one of the critical points of the conversation for
these young people was the idea that denominations may isolate us
from truths and fellowships present in other groups. The truths of God
may be represented in many faith traditions. No one group or sect
has a corner on that truth. The students represented at M7 rightly acknowledge that a divorce from fellowship with other groups can lead
to an insulated mentality that is not only insulated from risk, but that is
also insulated from growth.

The conversations then segued into the church's role in the political arena. One of the more pointed critiques leveled at the church in
this discussion was the evangelicalism's adoption of the Republican
Party as its party of choice. Many students expressed dismay and
frustration over this fact, lamenting that God does not ascribe to one
party or the other and that we can still have different opinions and different party allegiances and all be Christians.

"Church backs up the political right. If we want
our U.S. foreign policy to reflect Christ, it needs
to be dictated by love."

"Democrat or Republican, no president—good
or bad—will affect my Christianity."

"A lot of churches are way too patriotic. We've equated Christianity and nationalism. This has hurt us as we've related to the rest of the world."

"It would be helpful if the church leadership would educate lay people on how to think rightly about politics and issues that we often say are political."

"The church should not be silent when there is an obvious wrong."

"If we are not to kill and harm, what are we doing in those other countries?"

The students felt strongly that when the church becomes so entangled with a perspective, viewpoint, or position that it loses the ability to objectively and biblically engage that party in critique, it is in a volatile position. Not only does its entanglement with the world effectively silence every other member of a local or national church who would claim a diverse opinion, it also cuts short the church's ability to level prophetic criticism at the institution it has become beholden to.

Eugene Peterson warns of this danger in one of his latest works on spiritual theology, *Christ Plays in Ten Thousand Places*. He warns that the church placing leaders in prominent positions, and therefore gaining more acceptability as a faith, has no precedent in Scripture. In fact, he writes, "Eighteen hundred years or so of Hebrew history capped by a full exposition of Jesus Christ tell us that God's revelation of himself is rejected far more often than it is accepted, is dismissed by far more people than embrace it, and has been either attached or ignored by every major culture or civilization in which it has given its witness."[21] While we long as a church to maintain a biblical and Christological influence in our governments (both local and national), we must never be fooled into thinking that theocracy will work. C. S. Lewis once commented that each morning we should sit at the breakfast table with our Bibles and our local newspapers, our hearts tuned to both of our citizenships. From the discussion of these students, many feel that as a whole we have sacrificed our heavenly citizenship for a place at the table of the political right.

On the issue of tolerance, encountering differences and engaging diversity in our individual relationships were at the heart of this area of discussion. As with church at large, the students expressed a range of opinions on tolerance. Here, then, are some of their comments:

> "Understanding and empathy doesn't mean acceptance."

> "Some tolerance can appear to be apathy."

> "Loving the sinner and not the sin is hard to live."

> "September 11 brought along a lot of tolerance, including trying to understand where someone is coming from."

> "Tolerate is a bad word, because it implies obligation without love."

> "Tolerance may mean loving while not liking all that they are doing."

> "Love is our goal, not tolerance. Tolerance is one step below love. You can't just tolerate the poor and homeless, you have to love them."

"Be willing to listen and hear the other person's story. Accept the person; don't preach. Give them an opportunity to explain."

Perhaps these students, and many other church members, would be enlightened by more diverse experiences. Sadly, after coming to faith, we often segregate our lives into walled divisions of church activity and secular activity. While we must maintain jobs and other connections with the "outside world," we limit significant relationships to those who are like us, our "holy huddle" if you will. William G. Perry discusses this notion in his book, *Forms of Intellectual and Ethical Development in the College Years: A Scheme.* He points to the fact that many young adults never have enough diverse encounters to grow out of the black-and-white worldview they have as children and adolescents.

Their first encounters with multiplicity send many of them into a black-and-white mode of thinking that welcomes no other opinions. Rather, it retreats into a sheltered world that welcomes only the like-minded. In fact, both Perry and James Fowler (*Stages of Faith and Religious Development*) note that many adults have never left that stage of faith maturity in which the world is governed by a set of rules that have only black and white dimensions. Indeed, few of the concepts we encounter on a daily basis have such defined borders. In matters that are biblically clear—such as salvation by faith in Jesus Christ or other apradigms in the Christian faith—we must maintain our absolute adherence. But in many other areas of life there are no such prescriptions given in Scripture. In these matters, encounters with diversity may well lead us to new insight and deeper apprehension of the truth.

Many students expressed the desire, whether in support of tolerance or in critique of tolerance, that individually we portray the attributes of Jesus Christ. These comments suffused the entire discussion and point again to the overarching desire of twentysomethings to be involved in communities of faith that are authentically Christlike, and that foster intergenerational relationships.

One of the essential elements of this type of community is that each and every individual involved needs to be personally committed to godly living in their own lives. They must tend the fire within their own souls. When the Creek Nation of Native Americans was removed from the state of Florida, they carried their fire with them. It was the job of certain members of the tribe to never let the fire go out. So, the day they left their homes in the southeast, they carried the still-smoldering coals from their fires with them. They used these coals to start a new fire when they stopped on the first night of their forced journey. The next morning, they picked up the coals and guarded them throughout the day, using those protected coals to start the fire that night. They did this all the way to Georgia, where they were allowed to live several more years. When they were then removed from this land to the Oklahoma Territory, they again brought the fire with them.

The story of the Hebrews' exodus from Egypt contains a similarly powerful image. God instructed the children of Israel that on their journey through the wilderness, they were not to pack away the ark of the covenant like they did with all the other accoutrements of the tabernacle. The ark represented the presence of God among them and it was to be carried "on their shoulders," not pushed in front of them, nor pulled behind them, but on their physical bodies they were to bear the presence of God.

The students at the M7 conference expressed a deep desire to be in a community in which each member "brings her own fire." They long to engage in meaningful work that is both related to the lives of those around them, as well as meaningful to those outside the community to whom they reach out. These kinds of communities don't just happen. They are born from individuals who carry a fire within them that is tended in the daily work of living in communion with the one true God. In the end, the appearance of the church in twenty years will depend on these students and whether or not they have been welcomed and mentored and discipled in their communities of faith. As one student said, "It won't matter what the church looks like, it will matter what it does."

## What's Going On? Emerging Conversations in a Global City

By Gabriel and Jeanette Salguero

Here we are—a young evangelical married couple pastoring in New York City and feeling the energy of "new" conversations. Imagine with us an ongoing conversation about Christianity, culture, global crisis, and faith. This conversation is erupting among Christians all over the world. (Truth be told, this is not new, it's just a reemergence of themes that many Christians have always found important. The difference now is that broader coalitions of younger Evangelicals are part of the dialogue and the conversation is receiving attention from an entirely new constituency.) We want to underline that we, and many within our generation, place a heavy emphasis on *conversation*. By now you may be wondering, *What is everybody talking about?* Simply put, all around the United States, young Evangelicals[22]—Nazarenes included—are asking the questions: How can we be faithful witnesses of Jesus Christ in our generation? What models of leadership, evangelism, ministry, and worship would empower us to be effective while not compromising our message?

Many of the members and seekers who visit The Lamb's Church of the Nazarene in New York City have asked, "What is the relationship of your church with the larger city culture?" Certainly, this is not a new question. We take being witnesses in our time and place seriously. That is the reason why we must talk about Christianity and its relationship with postmodernity.[23] The postmodern conversation is just rephrasing that deep philosophical question raised by renowned singer-songwriter, Marvin Gaye, in his now famous, and often covered song, "What's Going On?"

Pastoring a church in Manhattan with a significant mixture of twentysomethings and recently arrived Latino and Asian immigrants has moved us to keep asking the question concerning faith and our contemporary culture. Jeanette and I have been asking these questions to ourselves for sometime. In addition, generations of pastors, leaders, theologians, and activists have asked the same query. Only now do we wrestle with postmodernity and its questioning of meta-narratives and absolutes; its valuing of multiple voices and pluralism; and its challenge to modern assumptions of the triumph of science, reason, logic, and power, among other things.

Joanne and Suri Singh, a teacher and a social worker in their late twenties and members of The Lamb's, are both great snapshots of these conversations. Joanne asks the query, "What is The Lamb's doing concerning Darfur and Rwanda? How can we launch ministry initiatives that speak and act intentionally and explicitly against this genocide?" In many ways Joanne and Suri are a microcosm of what the twentysomethings (and many others from different generations) are pushing the church to be—a spiritually-powerful, missional church that will try new methods of being church. The questions of Darfur, HIV and AIDS, genocide, and social justice are not distinct from our spiritual journey. They are at the center of our spiritual formation as Christians. Our friend and author, Brian McLaren, gets to the heart of this matter in his new book *Everything Must Change* when he clearly articulates in a myriad of ways the fundamental questions raised at The Lamb's: "What do the life and teachings of Jesus have to say about the most critical global problems in our world today?"[24]

What about Rachael and Chris Harrington, an artist and professional photographer who feel that their evangelism and worship should be reflected through their art, graphic designs, and photography? The Lamb's has a long history of engaging the arts, theater, and ministry outside the proverbial box. Is there not something redeemable in the arts that is God-given and that can be used for worship and outreach? Rachael, Chris, and so many others are part of the pulse of a radically-inclusive worship-evangelism that seeks to embrace the aesthetic. Recently, Jon Benitez, a Grammy winning artist, said he wants to minister to Jazz artists in New York. Many of these gifted musicians can't or won't come to church because they work on weekends or late Saturday nights. So Jon's thought is to hold jam sessions in the clubs with a Christian message, where we can then disciple them. This is a key component in postmodern missions—*meeting people where they are*. So here we go, preaching and teaching in a Jazz club. In many ways, postmoderns also seek to redeem much of the practices of early Christianity, namely, using all our gifts to the glory of God. Yeah, so some of these artists and creative individuals have the word redemption tattooed on their forearms (these are actual people attending The Lamb's) or are night owls or recluses. Still, they are our mission field and neighbors.

Perhaps the key expression of this conversation at The Lamb's is the phrase "the multivocality of the church." Multivocality is our commitment to multiple voices, stories, and people. This commitment has served us well on the Lower East Side of Manhattan. The Lower East Side is where trendy SoHo meets Chinatown, Little Italy, NYU, and a large Spanish community. Our geography and sense of mission dictate that we respect the multiplicity of God's creation ethnically, generationally, economically, and linguistically. Homogeneity is not what we're about (it has its place, but not in increasingly diversified communities all over the country). This multivocality is not easy (patience and cultural sensitivity to others are essential) but it is a sign of the kingdom of God. Besides, we don't always do things because they work; we do them because they are correct.

So what are we learning about the postmodern emergent church? What are these conversations revealing? What learnings about being church and doing mission can the postmoderns bring to our conversation? In short, "What matters?"

### Questions Matter (An Inquiring Faith)

Questions matter. This is something all the twentysomethings in my context keep telling me, "Don't forget to keep asking questions." Socrates once said, "An unexamined life is not worth living." Examining faith is not just a Socratic method, it is a profoundly New Testament practice. The New Testament gives importance to questioning and examination. Before the Christological revelation, Jesus himself leads with a question, "Who do you say that I am?" When Jesus was found in the temple as an adolescent it was said of Him, "He was listening and asking questions." For this group of Christians, the questions are just as critical as the answers, perhaps even more important. What if we're providing answers to questions no one is asking? The questions push us to make our Christianity relevant and missional for the sake of Christ.

### Issues Matter (A Social-Justice Faith)

A faith that does not seek to respond to the issues of its time risks becoming irrelevant. So when the congregation hears about AIDS in our city, or the gentrification that is displacing hundreds of individuals, people want to know, "What are we going to do about it?" The postmoderns want to make a difference. This is not idealism but Christian hope that Christ has empowered His church to transform the world and make disciples. We understand that if we ignore the real challenges of pandemics, genocide, poverty, and inequity we are not proclaiming a liberative and transformative gospel. If we don't listen to the cry of the city and nations they will not listen to our gospel message.

*Voices and People Matter (An Inclusive Community and Organic Leadership)*

People want to be heard! What a revelation! The postmoderns are very suspicious of hierarchical and authoritarian models of leadership. They welcome, you guessed it, conversation. What we have learned is you can have authority and influence without being authoritarian. Collective wisdom and dialogue takes time but is critical for affirming dignity and mutual respect. No, we don't always agree about decisions that have to be made, but the process of dialogue always creates room for feelings of good will. We are learning to continually put people and their voices ahead of wanting to be in charge.

Our prayer is that our journey as pastors would draw some insights for further discussion. As genuine disciples of Christ, we do not pretend that these are the last words; rather, they are some initial musings that would invite our church family to continue the conversation. We know we can't fix all of the problems, but we want God's will to be done on earth as it is in heaven. We're hopeful, not in human ability, but in a Holy-Spirit-empowered ministry that transforms our generation.

# Food for Thought

What is the purpose of denomination in today's society? Does it serve any purpose anymore? If so, has the denomination effectively made its distinctiveness so well known that society understands and accepts it? What is the church's stance on issues that are norms in society? Is the church tolerant in a positive way? Or has the church's view of tolerance actually painted it in a bad light? Has the church's members become so accepting of society that the world sees no difference between members of the church and the rest of society? If there is no viewable difference, what must the church do to show society there is a reason to become a part of the Body of Christ?

# Chapter 6
# Compassion and Justice

## Insights on Compassion and Justice
From Sarah Bechtold

*Sarah positions herself in the overstuffed chair to my right and smooths her long, wavy brown hair. She seems uncomfortable, nervous, as if she is applying for a job. Unlike some of my other interviewees, Sarah didn't know I had planned on interviewing her until she arrived. She hasn't had much time to think through her opinions. She doesn't even know what subject I will be discussing with her; nonetheless, she is willing to share her thoughts.*

*Having had the opportunity to be in a number of meetings with this young woman, I know she has a breadth of knowledge. Her husband is a student at Nazarene Theological Seminary, preparing for the pastorate. She is the assistant events coordinator at Nazarene Youth International (NYI). With NYI's growing involvement in projects that focus on social justice, Sarah undoubtedly has a certain perspective on these issues that the church needs to hear. I give her some background on this project and finally let her know what I want to talk to her about.*

*"Well, I'm not sure how much my opinion counts," she says with earnest modesty, "but I'm more than willing to let you know what I think if that's what you want."*

I smile. "Well of course I want your opinion, and of course it counts. I wouldn't have asked if I didn't."

"Alright, let's go for it," she says.

"Great! So, tell me, what are your first thoughts on the church and the issues of social justice?"

Sarah clears her throat, readjusts her position in the chair, and says, "I think the church would ideally like to bring justice into the world, but a lot of churches are too afraid to get their hands dirty in order to do that."

"Why do you think they're afraid to get their hands dirty?"

"I don't know," Sarah responds, contemplating for a brief moment. "When I think of people being afraid to get their hands dirty it's like standing up for the rights of human beings, whether you agree with them or not. Christians are afraid to walk up to the homeless person on the street. They're afraid to take a political stand for human rights. It's just too messy and too complicated for them."

"Do you feel like the church as a whole is too busy? Is that what you're saying? Or they can't be bothered with getting their hands dirty whether they need to or not?" I ask.

"They'd like to say that they are concerned, but it's too scary for them to get into that because the public opinion of them might be skewed. It's like 'Oh, no! They let homeless people go to that church. I can't go there.' I mean, I know there are a lot of churches that are very good with bringing about social justice, but as a whole I don't see that as a common thing." Sarah subconsciously strokes aside a lock of her bangs that has fallen down before her eyes. Then she continues.

"The other thing is churches that are spending millions and millions of dollars on church buildings that are really pretty when that millions of dollars could be used to completely redefine a country."

I'm intrigued by that comment, so I dig for more. "Why does that bother you personally?"

"'Cause I don't need to sit in a really pretty building to worship God. We were ordered to take care of the poor and the widows and it seems to me that money could be better used in areas of doing just that versus paying for a really pretty building. It just really bothers me that it's all about the church building fund instead of helping aid people in third-world countries. But 'Oh, no! We don't want to help those who have AIDS because that's their own fault.' You know what I mean?"

I nod my understanding and then take a different tact. "The church in North America is going to follow what the leaders call them to do. What do you think the leadership needs to do in order to change that mentality?"

"I think a lot of leaders—at least the ones I come into contact with—feel like they need to do more, but they know that if they push something like that in their church they'd probably have people leave. So I think church leaders might just need to get a backbone and say 'You know what? You might not agree with us needing to do this versus a church building project or a big production at Easter, but we're doing it anyway.' Don't get me wrong. Easter productions are important, but do we really need to spend so much on them? You can have an incredible Easter service without spending lots and lots of money on stage sets and really nice costumes and such. I don't know how much money goes into something like that, but it seems like a lot. They're just huge productions that take up our money, when we could do something else that could really change lives."

"Do you think your generation is going to be the one to change the church back to this perspective? And if they can't, what will their reaction be?

*"I sure hope so,"* she answers with a sigh of concern. *"I've talked to lots of young adults and teenagers and they really want to see something happen. They say they are really disappointed in what their church is doing and not doing. If they don't see a movement toward social justice happening, I think the church is going to lose a lot of people. For them, social justice is more important than attending church on Sunday."*

## Roundtable Discussion Overview

Compassion and justice are foundational tenets of Evangelicalism. And yet, many of the younger denominations birthed under this umbrella have experienced the same kind of atrophy that precipitated their departure from mainline sects near the turn of the twentieth century. As the Pentecostal and Evangelical movements have become more institutionalized, it is apparent that they have often abandoned their connections with minorities and the less fortunate who made up the core of their adherents at the outset. This institutional phenomenon boils under the surface of this chapter's discussion. The questions in this section of the discussion precipitated a response from students who are critical of this disconnection and long to be involved in a Christian faith community that actively embraces the weak, poor, and disadvantaged.

But in the last decade, the Evangelical church has become increasingly good at building wealth and at the same time abandoning social involvement, leaving it to government welfare and secular charitable organizations to meet the needs of the poor and oppressed. Even though providing for the needy was a mark of early Evangelicalism, the twentieth century has seen a flourishing of prosperity movements that removed the focus from the poor and turned the church's gaze on its own needs and desire for wealth. This teaching comes dangerously close to abandoning the poor and oppressed who are not appropriating God's blessings through right behavior. A constellation of factors—including prosperity teaching, racism and prejudices, and facilities proximity—has caused a withdrawal of many congregants from the work that Jesus spent most of His time on earth doing: healing the sick, feeding the hungry, and declaring freedom to those in bondage. As one student commented during our discussion, "We depend way too much on the government to do what the church should be doing."

The questions posed at the beginning of this discussion on compassion and justice were:

- **What is poverty (U.S. and global)? How should Christians respond to poverty?**

- **What responsibility does the church in America have in addressing poverty worldwide?**

- **What are the most significant social issues facing your city? The world?**

- **How does your local church encourage or build community?**

- **How should Christians respond to the HIV/AIDS crisis?**

Students, many of whom have been members of local congregations for their entire lives, called for an integrated engagement of the issues that plague much of humanity outside American borders. Here are some of their comments about the suffering of the world:

"Jesus was always among the poor."

"End it."

"Sometimes you have to deal with the source of the problems so that the problems don't keep happening, i.e., drug programs, etc. Looking at the person as a whole person, not just as a drug addict."

"Not only say we are going to do something, we have to actually do it."

"We have to equip other nations to get out of poverty."

"Maybe we shouldn't support killing people but should feed people and supply water instead. People might not be mad at you if you feed them, clothe them, or give them water, rather than shoot them and blow their country up."

While many students commented on the church's responsibility to address the poverty and suffering of the world, many also noted that the church has not accepted this responsibility outside our country's borders, let alone within our own cities. The work of churches in international mission efforts proves to be suspect when it is not coupled with outreach to the poor and the lost right outside our own front doors. The following comments show the inauthentic witness these students have noticed as our churches often fail to reach out to those in poverty on our doorsteps:

"American culture isn't really embracing compared to cultures around the world. So, we can go overseas, but we don't want them living next to us."

"The church sends people overseas, but ignores the needs at home."

"Many churches are blind to the poverty around us and are looking at global poverty."

"We have the responsibility to bless others with what we have been given and to increase the understanding of our situations and those of others."

"It's difficult to talk about poverty and economic injustice when the extent of our solutions entails simply writing a check."

"Americans don't know what being defeated or oppressed is really about, so we can barely define poverty."

The issue of poverty was raised again and again as students conversed about compassion and justice. The students' comments ranged from a critique of their own generation for spending more money at Starbucks than on donations for the poor to the naming of other issues such as AIDS, homosexuality, and immigration as concerns that the church should be addressing:

"So many ways to serve, but we would rather buy coffee at Starbucks than a five dollar shirt for someone who needs it."

"Regarding the AIDS pandemic, there needs to be more education awareness, more knowledge about it as a global problem."

"Immigrants—step up and help them."

"If people have HIV, do not judge or ask or condemn. Listen to their stories, love them, value them, and allow them to be free."

Some students noted specific programs at their universities and in their local communities that they felt followed Jesus' model in ministering with compassion and justice. Many more described opportunities that existed, but that had been ignored or abandoned by local congregations. Here are some of the problems students identified as specific to their local communities, as well as some compassionate and socially-engaged models that are working in their universities and churches:

"MNU (MidAmerica Nazarene University) is currently working on an AIDS project as a community."

"In Toledo we have a major problem of sex trafficking."

"Cincinnati sees a lot of drugs and violence."

"Nashville has a huge amount of drugs, prostitution, and homelessness."

"In Lansing, the most significant social issue facing our city is the loss of jobs due to the closing of factories."

"There are gangs everywhere. At NNU (North-western Nazarene University), we had three murders near campus in one week."

"Racism is rampant in Canada. There is no respect for other ethnic groups, especially the French and English."

"Our town is 50 percent Hispanic. It feels like our church holds this community at arms length. We're too passive. There is a language barrier, yes, but there's a need for mixing."

"The church tried to hand out clean needles to help stop spread of HIV. The dirty needles are collected so they aren't passed around and reused."

Remarkably, many of these quotes highlight the problem of racism that continues to exist in local communities. Other students commented that while they would not call their local congregations racist, they are not yet welcoming to other ethnic groups or races. Many mentioned that their churches are suspicious of those who attend from diverse groups, those who do not resemble the majority of the congregation.

A significant complication of this issue concerns the geographical location of local churches. Some students leveled a critique at the church because of its departure from the neighborhoods and inner city areas where the poor, and increasingly diverse ethnic or cultural groups, are often represented. This departure leaves neighborhoods unchurched due to the congregation's decision to relocate to more suburban, and often more affluent, areas of metropolitan centers. Furthermore, this relocation demands that churches spend more of their treasure on new buildings and facilities when they do relocate. Consequently, they are not able to respond to needs, even when they are in a position to see them. These two details combine to create a negative perspective to the students who were part of this discussion. This urban flight has not been lost on students who believe the church has not shouldered its responsibility for the inner city:

> "I think we're called to follow Jesus—to feed the hungry, visit people in prison, be friends with the homeless. I think that's what all Christians need to do, and though we have specific ministries for that, we haven't done that as believers."

> "We need to be more intentional in urban areas because of the way society has progressed outside of the city. Proximity is so important to how you minister; if you're moving or commuting all the time, you can't establish relationships."

> "We are disappointed in churches leaving areas of plight and going to new suburban areas."

> "There are huge churches with not much outreach happening."

> "Poverty, from our viewpoint, is almost surreal until you see it in person. We have removed ourselves from it."

> "We are only willing to help those we can fix. There is no mention made of the mentally ill, the

immigrants, the homosexuals—those who do not fit into our lives so readily."

In the final analysis, students rightly asserted that to deal with poverty and other global issues and to provide justice for those who are oppressed in all parts of our world, the church must *be* the church and build relationships one person at a time.

The twentysomething students demonstrated once again their own authentic faith as they cry for mentoring relationships that not only increase their spiritual maturity but that also allow all of us to grow into genuine Christlikeness. They recognized that growth in faith comes through the inner working of the Holy Spirit and through the grace and mercy modeled by believers who come alongside them. And in this manner, they will be equipped to serve and comfort generously.

## Community: Where Wholeness Is Restored
By Althea C. Taylor

Imagine that you are walking through a city in the United States or Canada. What do you see? How do you feel? Perhaps you're able to see, beyond the lights and the attractions of the city, the abject poverty in the shadows of the hustle and bustle. You may see the homeless scouring for food in trash receptacles or hovering in dark corners for shelter. Perhaps you notice the alarming number of children who seem to be engulfed in this picture as they panhandle for money. Perhaps you feel a sense of hopelessness, despair, anger, or utter frustration. Just as quickly as these emotions come, you look out of the corner of your eye and notice a church. Suddenly you have a glimmer of hope. You are inspired as you think that surely there is someone in this community who cares about these conditions and is doing something to help. Isn't there?

Statistics alarmingly tell us that in North America, 12.8 million children are living in poverty.[25] Millions in our labor force are falling closer to the poverty line, as the gap between the haves and the have-nots widens. And the number of severely poor has grown by 26 percent. Where does the church stand on these issues? Is this the church's problem? Is this not the role of the government to care for these issues? As the debate continues, the conditions worsen, and I believe God is taking notes on our response.

God's strategy for transforming the world is the church. The church is not only about justification but also about rectification, challenging and changing the culture of a world void of God into a culture and society that operates according to the principles of God. The church is the people of God: those who identify with and proclaim Jesus Christ as sovereign Lord. The church is more than a social service organization; it is called to be a life-transforming organization. In John 17, Jesus prays first for himself, then His disciples, and finally for those who would believe because of the testimony of His disciples. More specifically, in verse 23, Jesus prays that the world would know that Jesus was sent by God and that He loves the world. This prayer is significant because it compels the church—you and I who are followers of Christ—to bring a message of relevance to a world without God. If the church has been given this message, then we must be a part of God's strategy for reaching those who have yet to realize why Christ is essential to their lives; why Christ cares about their human condition; why Christ is concerned about their hunger, poverty, brokenness, hurts, and despair.

St. Francis of Assisi is quoted as saying, "preach always, and if necessary, use words." Jesus demonstrated His love for us through compassion, and the second chapter of Philippians depicts His humility and compassion. He became what we are so that through Him we might become as He is. In *Compassion,* Henri Nouwen explains where compassion asks us to go:

To go where it hurts, to enter into places of pain, to share in brokenness, fear, confusion, and anguish. Compassion challenges us to cry out with those in misery, to mourn with those who are lonely, to weep with those in tears. Compassion requires us to be weak with the weak, vulnerable with the vulnerable, and powerless with the powerless. Compassion means full immersion in the condition of being human.

Most people consider themselves to be compassionate: basically good, gentle, and understanding. We tend to have a natural response to human suffering: the poor old man, the hungry child, the homeless individual or family, the paralyzed soldier. But compassion is more than a good response to human suffering. As the Church, we are called to live counter-cultural in love and service. *We move from positions of comfort to embrace those within our community who are marginalized.* We are called to suffer with them and advocate on their behalf and demolish unjust practices that perpetuate human suffering. The Church is called to curb the power of Satan in this world until the Kingdom of God is fully established with good conquering evil as God intended.[26]

The church is called to live and operate according to the principles of the communities; communities where people can be reconciled to Christ and to others. In a healing community, the mind of Christ is manifested and our lives become compassionate because of the way we live and work together. We transcend our individual limitations and develop a concrete realization of the self-emptying of Christ because we have a deep sense of being gathered by God. In healing communities, we forego judgment and experience forgiveness. Problems that would overburden and cripple an individual become surmountable when faced by a community of believers dependent upon God. We become a unified voice and model life according to God's principles. We begin to experience a community where there is no hunger among us, where children are loved and educated, and where wealth is not reserved for the privileged but is utilized to minimize the gap between the haves and have-nots.

In community, we meet the whole needs of humanity: spiritual, physical, emotional, financial, and psychological. In community, wholeness is restored to that which God intended.

## Food for Thought

What has happened to take the church to such a level that most congregations have little, if anything, to do with issues of social justice? Is it important for the church to be about the business of being an advocate for social justice? Is there a fear amongst the members of local congregations to get their hands dirty, as described by the interviewee in this chapter? What practices must the church adopt to reshape itself as an organization that meets the needs of the lonely, the lost, the left out, the sick, the dying, and the least? What are the consequences of such a change?

# Epilogue
# The Response

So what is the response of the church to these observations by twentysomethings? Does the leadership of the church take them seriously? Or does it view the observations of its young adult population as ramblings of a dissatisfied generation simply wishing to complain? If they are taken seriously, then there are a number of serious indictments that must be addressed.

The issues of intergenerational relationships and ministry cropped up repeatedly during the discussions. Since that is so, shouldn't these be addressed in some manner by the local congregation? In creating avenues for intergenerational relationships, how will the local congregation tear down the walls of separation it has created with the hope of more effectively ministering to particular age-groups, and instead create avenues for relationship, discipleship, and koinonia? Certainly this will mean reshaping the structure of ministry for many congregations. But so will it likely mean healthier congregations in the long run.

Regarding the call for social justice—another subject that surfaced regularly—maybe the question isn't whether the church can do more, but how will it do more? If the foundations of the Church of the Nazarene were rooted in ministry to the poor, lonely, and the outcasts of society, should not each congregation at least be asked to reevaluate their efforts with the hope that more can be accomplished?

What of the charge that leadership is not effectively recognizing the call of the laity as effectively as it recognizes the call of the pastors into ministry? Certainly no one would agree that this is a standing policy in the church. However, for it to have been pointed out repeatedly gives validity to the idea that the practice exists. What exactly has been the effect on ministry efforts of this tradition? And what must be done to change that convention in the future?

What of the questions regarding effective discipleship, purity training, community involvement, or positive outreach? Each of the issues is multifaceted with no easy solutions. But each must be grappled with if the church is to advance the Kingdom.

And so, leadership has a massive task set before them. It is true that not every congregation will be able to address all of these subjects. Some may not even be addressable. However, to make no effort at all would be a travesty, especially when addressing these issues starts simply with prayer and conversations. And in this effort, may the Holy Spirit guide the church in all it does.

# Questions Proposed for Round Table Discussions

## Personal Growth

How does the church stay connected to your generation?

Is the holiness message still relevant? What is the holiness message in your eyes?

How does a Christian mature spiritually?

What is the "role of authority" of Scripture?

## Lifestyle

What is Christian purity when it comes to lifestyle and sexuality?

How is a Christian lifestyle distinct from a non-Christian lifestyle?

Are there behaviors that Christians need to avoid? Why?

Are there behaviors that Christians need to authenticate within their lifestyle? Why?

## Ministry and Calling

Describe your understanding of calling.

How do you plan to live out your ministry or your calling?

What does it mean to be missional?

## Church and Community

What is the role of the local church in your life?

What do you see as your role in the life of the local church?

What are the things you think the church is very concerned about that it shouldn't be?

What is most effective way to introduce your age-group to Jesus?

What are you doing to address social issues in your city?

Does the church have the authority to tell you anything?

Does the church have authority?

How should we respond to leaders in the church?

## Church and Society

Is denomination important?

How do you feel about the American evangelical church and U.S. foreign policy?

Describe the dynamics of the changing culture in and out of the church.

What are a few ways you can impact the local and global church?

How do you define tolerance?

What is the church in twenty years?

## Compassion and Justice

What is poverty (U.S. and global)? How should Christians respond to poverty?

What responsibility does the church in America have in addressing poverty worldwide?

What are the most significant social issues facing your city? The world?

How does your local church encourage or build community?

How should Christians respond to the HIV/AIDS crisis?

# About the Authors

**David and Rhonda Dean Kyncl** serve as the directors of the 2:8 House, a ministry of the Church of the Nazarene on the University of Oklahoma campus. David also serves as the director of Nazarene Secular Campus Missions in the United States and Canada. Rhonda is writing her dissertation in pursuit of a Ph.D. in English Composition, Rhetoric and Literacy at OU. They both teach freshman classes on campus. The Kyncls have two children, Mary and Jonathan, and are actively involved with their local congregation—Norman Community Church of the Nazarene. (You can e-mail them at kyncl@28house.org.)

**Jeff Edmondson** is the Publishing Manager of Barefoot Ministries, the youth publishing division of Nazarene Publishing House (NPH). Prior to this position, Jeff served as the Youth Program Editor for NPH. Jeff has also served as the Pastor to Families & Youth at Harrisonburg First Church of the Nazarene, in Harrisonburg, Virgina, and has written hundreds of articles and five books, including his most recent two— *Gutsy Faith: Hard Conversations with God* and *The Grind: Living a "God-life" in the Real World.* Jeff lives in Lee's Summit, Missouri, with his wife, Cheri, and their two sons, Logan and Brady.

# Notes

1. Wikipedia describes the Millennials, or Generation Y, as those born between 1982 and 1994. Wikipedia contributors, "Generation Y," *Wikipedia, The Free Encyclopedia,* <http://en.wikipedia.org/w/index.php?title=Generation_Y&oldid=237707798>. For another helpful source for understanding the characteristics of this generation, see "Who are the Millenials?" *Deloitte,* <http://www.deloitte.com/dtt/cda/doc/content/us_consulting_milennialfactsheet_080606.pdf>.

2. Tom Nees, letter to all Nazarene college and university presidents in the United States and Canada, October 3, 2005.

3. Tom Nees, e-mail message to a college chaplain, October 30, 2005.

4. The Barna Group, "Most Twentysomethings Put Christianity on the Shelf Following Spiritually Active Teen Years," <http://www.barna.org/FlexPage.aspx?Page=BarnaUpdate&BarnaUpdateID=245>.

5. A complete list of these topics and questions is available in the Appendix.

6. "Spirituality in Higher Education," Higher Education Research Institute, UCLA, <http://www.spirituality.ucla.edu/index.html>.

7. The Barna Group.

8. Walter Brueggemann, *The Cadences of Home: Preaching to Exiles* (London: Westminster John Knox Press, 1997), 44.

9. C. S. Lewis, *Mere Christianity* (New York: Macmillan Publishing, 1980), 171.

10. Kenda Creasy Dean and Ron Foster, *The Godbearing Life: The Art of Soul Tending for Youth Ministry* (Nashville: Upper Room Books, 1998), 31.

11. The Barna Group.

12. St. John of the Cross, *Dark Night of the Soul,* as quoted in *Devotional Classics,* eds. Richard Foster and James Bryan Smith (New York: HarperCollins Publishers, 1990), 34.

13. Rob Bell, *Sex God: Exploring the Endless Connections Between Sexuality and Spirituality* (Grand Rapids, Mich.: Zondervan, 2008), 123.

14. Os Guinness, *The Call: Finding and Fulfilling the Central Purposes of Your Life* (Nashville: Thomas Nelson, 2003), 4.

15. Steve Shadrach, *The Fuel and the Flame: 10 Keys to Ignite Your Campus for Jesus Christ* (Fayetteville, Ark.: The BodyBuilders, 2003), 89.

16. Guinness, *The Call,* 31-2, 38.

17. Brian D. McLaren, *More Ready Than You Realize* (Grand Rapids, Mich.: Zondervan, 2002), 123.

18. Ibid, 84-5.

19. For more information on *Kaleo,* visit <www.kaleocommunity.org>.

20. For information on Blood:Water Mission, visit <http://www.blood watermission.com>.

21. Eugene Peterson, *Christ Plays in Ten Thousand Places: A Conversation in Spiritual Theology* (Grand Rapids, Mich.: William B. Eerdmans Publishing Company, 2005), 288.

22. A great summary of the worldview of younger evangelicals (mostly in the United States) can be found by reading Robert E. Webber's *The Younger Evangelicals: Facing the Challenges of the New World* (Grand Rapids, Mich.: Baker Books, 2002).

23. For a fuller and better theological treatise on postmodernity and the church, see Stanley Grenz's *A Primer on Postmodernism* (Grand Rapids, Mich.: William B. Eerdmans Publishing Company, 1996). We argue that postmodernity presents challenges and promises for the redeeming parts of culture, such as law, education, medicine, technology, and art.

24. Brian D. McLaren, *Everything Must Change: Jesus, Global Crises, and a Revolution of Hope* (Nashville: Thomas Nelson, 2007), 12.

25. Children's Defense Fund, "Child Poverty in America," <http://www.childrensdefense.org/site/DocServer/Child_Poverty_in_America_Sept_2007.pdf?docID=4941>.

26. Henri Nouwen, *Compassion: A Reflection on the Christian Life* (New York: Doubleday Dell Publishing Group, Inc., 1982), 4.